To Brian

A Practical Guide to
Making Spirituality Understandable

Finding Your Soul

At Work At Home,
and
When You're Alone!

Eight Clues to Creating a Happy,
More Satisfying Life

Frank Robinson

by

Frank Robinson and Elio Agostini

Finding Your Soul

At Work at Home,
and
When You're Alone!

For information contact:

Agostini - Robinson, LLC

PO Box 10581 Bainbridge Island, WA 98110

FindingYourSoul.com

Second Edition

This edition published by Magicstone Media

Book cover design by Lisa Agostini

ISBN 0-9770205-0-9

Library of Congress Control Number 2005908857

Table of Contents

Chapter One
A Practical Guide To Spirituality..............................*1*

Chapter Two
Looking For The Answers.................................*11*

Chapter Three
Suffering Is A Gift In Disguise.............................*21*

Chapter Four
Live Your Life In Each Moment Of Now......................*39*

Chapter Five
Learn To Choose Soul Over Ego, Love Over Fear.............*55*

Chapter Six
Practice Loving Yourself *75*

Chapter Seven
Be Honest With Yourself In All Things......................*95*

Chapter Eight
Let Go Of Attachment To Outcome *109*

Chapter Nine
Forgiveness: A Gift That Transforms The Giver............. *133*

Chapter Ten
Practice Some Form Of Meditation...................... *153*

Chapter Eleven
Epilogue *173*

Acknowledgments

Frank Robinson

I dedicate this book to Dr. John Enright. There is not a day, rarely an hour, that goes by that I do not use the ideas and material I learned from working with John. His contribution to my understanding of how human experience is 'wired up' has been immense. John was a brilliant man and a bright soul.

I want to thank Ram Dass for his influence on my spiritual journey. He helped me learn how to relate lovingly *to* my ego rather than fearfully *from* it. I never met a man who was so willing to tell on himself. I have never had an interaction with him in which I did not learn something that changed my life in an expanding way.

I want to thank Elio Agostini, my co-author. This book would not have been written if it were not for Elio. He has been and continues to be a close friend and a life changing influence on me. His incredible organizational skills and his tenacity have kept this project afloat. He pushes me deeper into my own personal experience and challenges me to articulate the ideas in down to earth terms. Writing a book with someone is a very intimate experience. Elio has become a close confidant, sharing our most challenging and most uplifting moments with each other. He has been a loving and constant inspiration to me.

I want to thank the friends and loved ones who have edited our book, believed in us and given us constant emotional support through the four years of writing and rewriting of our book. Mary Anderson has been a help mate, a true friend, a spiritual and religious teacher, an unyielding grammarian and one who provoked clarity and refinement to the ideas we wanted to deliver. She has also been an absolutely delightful dance partner, a chef extrodinaire and a loving companion. I don't know how I would have gotten through this without her. I want to thank Marie Annette Brown for her support and encouragement from the inception of this book. Her belief in me, the inspiration of her own spiritual journey of the last twenty five years and her generosity of heart have fed my soul. I want to thank Ann Marie Stacker for giving me a sense of family: kids, cats, dogs, fish, rabbits and all the chaos that comes with it. I am bigger for having her in my life. Her editorial input was grounding. Annie's belief in me and her continued friendship is a blessing to me. I want to thank Bill Shaul, Leo Pocuis (I couldn't have written it without you, Bud) and Pat Barrett. A man could not possibly have truer friends. Thank you for sharing your lives and your families with me.

I want to thank Lisa Agostini, Elio's beautiful daughter. Perhaps more than any other single person Lisa lifted this book to another level. She designed and produced the book cover. Her editing of the content of our book was significant. She lovingly pushed us to explain some very complex ideas and experiences into understandable words and a story line that would feel familiar to anyone. Lisa helped make our book become more relevant, deeper and more touching. She has been a God send to us and we love and appreciate her.

I want to thank Angie and Mitch Henderson for their involvement in our project, their friendship and their unending support with our web site. I also want to thank our professional editors, Billie Judy and Jonathan Stratman. They forced us to hear our own words as a reader might. They have been there through several versions of the book and believed in what we were trying to do.

Thank you all.

— *Frank Robinson*

Elio Agostini

After thirty-five years of working in the publishing business, I was disenchanted with what I had seen in the business world and even more discouraged with the amount of suffering and stress I saw in many of my employees. I wanted to see if I could find some kind of answers and solutions to those who seemed disillusioned, isolated, scared, unappreciated and distrustful. My problem was that I was generally just as confused as everyone else. I needed help, too!

Four years ago it was my hopeful suggestion that Frank write this book with me. Thankfully he consented and the journey began for both of us.

My task in completing this book was to be the organizer, researcher and 'contrarian' to the theories and thoughts in the book. In other words, I am basically the fictitious character, William, in the book.

My struggles are discussed in great detail and I'm a little uncomfortable admitting it to you. The benefit of exposing myself with all my uncertainties and 'conditioned thoughts and feelings' is that I know that I'm not alone in my confusion. At this moment nearly one quarter of the adult population in the USA has been diagnosed with one form or the other of anxiety or depression.

This book is predominately Frank's approach to finding your soul. The content of this book is Frank's innovative, gentle and practical approach to understanding ourselves and the tools available to us on the healing spiritual journey we are all on, whether we are aware of it or not. I have read over 165 bestsellers on spirituality, self-help and motivational and inspirational theories, and I have never heard anyone talk about these principles the way my friend, Frank, does. Frank had been teaching and counseling his clients with these concepts for years and I am proud that I helped to give him the opportunity to pass it on to a greater number of people.

Frank has graciously thanked the people who were instrumental in our book being published and I endorse his thoughts and offer my sincere thanks as well. On a more personal level I would like to mention that I have been inspired in my life by a few special souls: Elise, for her determination and delightful approach to individuality; Melissa, for her unrelenting devotion to my happiness; Susan, whose suffering taught me an ever-expanding compassion; my dear

96 year-old mother, Norma, for her independence and perseverance; and my son, Miguel, for his strength and fortitude. In all they have greatly contributed to my life experience and influenced my thoughts and actions.

There is one other person that I feel deserves a special mention again. My sweet and courageous daughter, Lisa, not only contributed the design of the book but also read every line, and her comments and her thoughts frequently appear on our pages. She was magical, funny, insightful, concerned, comforting, intelligent and sensitive in her communications with us. Of course, none of this was surprising to her dear old dad, because that is exactly the traits she has exhibited throughout her life. I love you, Lisa, and I personally dedicate this book to you.

– *Elio Agostini*

Chapter One

A Practical Guide to Spirituality

Finding Your Soul At Work, At Home and When You're Alone! is a practical guide to making spirituality understandable and useful in every aspect of your life. It is intended to be an owner's manual to understanding yourself - without losing the mystery - a 'how-to' book offering a practical guide to spirituality and effective living. It is our interpretation of how human experience is basically 'wired up'.

There is a divinely inspired, soulful, spirit-based place inside all of us where we are always at peace, safe, secure, clear, strong, gentle and wise. If we are not experiencing those things in our life, it's not because they are not there. It's because we're not where they are!

We have heard no one talk about finding your soul the way we want to talk about it. The vision and experience of spirituality is clear for both of us. The Eight Clues we want to share with you are a result of where we now are in our lives, the sum of our experiences - how we each 'got here' and how we have thus far moved through our own suffering.

What we will share in this book is by definition beyond words. So our words are not meant to hand you truth on a silver platter, but rather to point you to a silver platter with which to embrace your own truth. We do not suggest that we have the 'right' answers for everyone. However, we have each personally found these spiritual tools profoundly useful and invite you to see if they resonate for you as well.

If they ring true for you, then you - and only you - will find ways to use these Eight Clues as an inspirational and practical guide to improve the quality of every aspect of your life - a happier and more passionate life!

We each wrote this book for ourselves, but for somewhat different reasons. Yet we agree that in our combined 65 years of business experience, consulting and counseling, no one has adequately dealt with spirituality and the emotions of daily living in a way that seems practical.

We invite you to temporarily suspend what might be your normal way of thinking about things and consider what we have to say here. If you are willing to do that, you'll learn some very practical pathways to discover or rediscover your spiritual self, to get off autopilot and realize the significance of the choices you make every day.

While it's human nature to want to know and understand, it seems to us that we have lost the sense of balance between knowing and experiencing or feeling things. Where are people supposed to go to learn why and how we feel the things we do?

We think that what we feel has more to do with the quality of our life than what we know. For instance, what if you finally knew everything and discovered you were still miserable?

Good news! The dynamics and mechanisms of human experience are accessible. This isn't magic. It's knowable and learnable. But where are the people and the classes to coach us and help us practice this stuff?

Wayne Dyer states: *"I tried to put together a curriculum in schools to train young people how to be the healthiest human beings they can be. You ask yourself what do you want for your kids? What's the answer? I want them to be happy! I don't want them to be neurotic. I want them to be fulfilled, I want them to have a sense of purpose in their lives. And where can they go to learn? Where are the courses on how to avoid feeling guilty, and how not to think anxiously, and how not to worry about what others think of you, how to eliminate approval-seeking all the time, and how to love yourself, and how to live in the present rather than live in the future or in the past?"*

We agree.

Actually, there are and have been a fair number of courses around. These are the personal growth seminars and workshops. And there are many religious paths that point to some of the principles we will cover. But none of them really focus on the spirit and mind/body connection in the way that we want to talk about it. They either tend to get stuck in psycho-babble or turn towards religious dogma. It's our intention to help you learn not just how to be temporarily happy but rather to help you discover where your happiness originates.

We have chosen to write this book because we also feel many of us have forgotten or have never really learned the practical guides to living a happy, healthy and soulful life.

Soul

When we speak of the 'soul' we refer to that aspect of our being, in fact, the very essence of our being, which connects us to all of life, each other, the earth and all its creatures and to the Source. We refer to the soul by using many words and phrases such as spirit, inner or higher self, deeper self, the heart, the loving witness within, the universal mind, the big mind. We consider soul to be our access point to the Divine, whatever you consider that to be.

The soul is beyond the realm of the intellect and the mind/body. It is not measurable in the science of physical reality. Soul is bigger than that. In fact, physical reality only exists in the context of the Divine. Through our soul, we all have access to a shared and very real experience of this Source. We may or may not be consciously aware of this 'connectedness' but it is nevertheless very real. It is, and we are part of, the Mystery.

Ego

When we speak of the ego we are referring to that part of us that thinks it is us. The value of the ego is that it is the mechanism by which the Source creates the unique and inescapable opportunities for each of us to do the healing work we came here to do. By its very nature it is always based in fear, scarcity and separation. It lives in a fear of loss of the infinite love from which it came. It is in a constant state of seeking or trying to hold onto enough love, money, sex, power, control and safety. It feels separate from everything and everybody. It feels it is different, alone and only knows to search for the love it needs out in the world of physical reality. The problem is, of course, that the world of physical reality doesn't make that love in the size package we need.

The ego is the source of all of our suffering. It creates its own suffering by forming attachments to the people, things, circumstances or objects it thinks might deliver the love, safety and connection for which it longs. It forms these attachments by fearful, insecure thoughts. Those thoughts are the source of the feelings that we call our suffering.

The ego is not the enemy or the problem in our lives. It is completely innocent and yet totally misguided in its experience of life. The problem is in those moments of now that we identify with our ego rather than our soul.

Life is a dance between the 'ego' and the 'soul', which continues every moment of our entire lives, whether we're aware of it or not. Who 'leads the dance' determines the quality of our life, moment to moment.

So how do we nurture our soul, allowing spirit to manage our life? There's the story about an old Native American tribal chief who, when asked how he would describe his own inner struggles, answered:

"There are two dogs inside me.
One of the dogs is mean and evil.
The other dog is good.
The mean dog fights the good dog all the time."
When he was asked which one wins, he answered,
"The one I feed the most."

America seems to have shifted to a 'left brain', ego-driven culture. The rational, scientific, logical thought process dominates and leads the charge to manipulate and control everything it can, which leads to chaos and misery. But when soul, rather than ego, manages our lives, the results are always positive and life-enhancing. With a payoff like that, isn't it worth the effort to make spirituality understandable and therefore, applicable to everyday living? The potential is mind-boggling.

We feel we are all strongly influenced by the 'corporate world' in which we live. By corporate world we mean all of the business world, from the front door to the boardroom. We are referring to every person that lives or works in the world of business. And who of us doesn't? Business in America and most of the rest of the world is a perfect reflection of how each of us lives our life. Therefore, we also think this applies to family, community, politics, religion, education and in our own personal life, especially when we are alone.

Today, so many of us are totally stressed-out. Most of us are obsessed with our jobs and holding on to them. We take the least amount of vacations of any society in the industrialized world. We seem to be in a constant search for more, more, more while worrying about the high cost of living. The demands from others never end. We move from one crisis to another and never have time for what really counts.

For the first time in American history, single people living alone outnumber traditional family households. We communicate with assorted electrical gadgets like cell phones, faxes, computers and the Internet instead of face-to-face. Even companies insulate themselves from us by using automated phone systems - efficient but soulless.

The outcome is that many of us have become disengaged, critical, afraid and out-of-touch with our souls. We've become isolated from other people and our sense of connection with the world around us.

In the past we could turn to our family, the church, our neighbors or our community to provide us with the focus in our day-to-day lives. For numerous reasons, many of us have lost contact with the love and support they can offer.

The most powerful force in our corporate world today is business. It seems to control our lives and has a major voice in how our world is being shaped. So how are we all feeling about how business is being conducted these days?

A Common Experience

Imagine you are a woman in your mid-thirties with two girls in public school, married to a man who is very busy running his own small business. You have some college education and you've just been promoted to middle-management. You are now on the fast track. You and your family just moved into a new house in a city away from your relatives and the friends you grew up with. You're doing the best you can but it never seems to be enough. Recently you've noticed you're often close to tears and you've been getting a lot of headaches. You're drinking too much coffee. You're feeling agitated, always in a rush. You feel like you have no time for yourself. You're wondering, "Is this all there is? Why do I feel so empty, alone and disconnected?"

This person has lost touch with her soul. And we're here to assure her that finding her soul is simple but it may not necessarily be easy for her to embark on that wonderful inward journey. This book is intended to offer her the tools needed for that journey. The adventure will be worth every moment of her time!

Getting There From Here

The quality of spirituality comes from within the very essence of your being. The answer does not lie 'out in the world'. There is nothing you have to do to get spirituality. Since it is your natural state of being, you access it by learning how to let go of the thoughts that pulled you away from your soul in the first place.

That's not an easy task! We all have deeply ingrained patterns of thoughts and beliefs that are difficult to release. But we can learn to more frequently cultivate spiritual experience. How? By learning ways to deepen our awareness of the practical wisdom of the Eight Clues, and using them.

Many speakers and authors are proponents of 'positive thinking' and their intention is right on target. But many of the theories that could be valuable and which are guaranteed to work, fail to get to the essence of the problem. They don't explain how to 'get there' - to feel positive from *the inside.*

Phil McGraw has written some wonderful and helpful books. If you watch Dr. Phil on television you know one of his favorite expressions is, "What the hell were you thinking?"

Reflect on this: your thinking does indeed determine your experience of life. The problem is not so much about controlling your thoughts but rather how to choose *where* those thoughts are coming from - your soul (love) or your ego (fear).

If you want your life to have value and meaning, where will you find the answers to your questions? We think the answers lie within the Eight Clues.

The first step is understanding who you are: a spiritual being living in the physical universe. Second, is discovering the tools and understanding the mechanics that will help you live in this world we've created.

The reason to get skilled at connecting with your deeper self is not that you'd be a better person - though it may feel that way. It's important to be clear on this: *there is nothing wrong with who you are at the core of your being.* It's just that who you are at the core of your being is not who most of us get to live with on a daily basis. So, the reason to tap into those 'core resources' is simply because *everything in your life works better in those moments that you live from your spiritual centeredness (soul) rather than from your reactive, off-centeredness (ego).*

You are the one who determines the quality of your life. The intent is to get to a point where *awareness* of what you're doing and what you are experiencing helps you make better choices. The blows we all take in this life can guide us to exactly where we have gotten stuck. As you learn to honor the process of awareness and letting life's blows be your guide, your life becomes more of a *soul-nurturing activity.*

If you can cultivate that awareness in a few more 'moments of now' each day, soon you might be feeling better 30 per cent of the time, then 40 per cent. If you can identify with your soul rather than your reactive self 50 per cent of the time or more, then the stuff that happens the rest of the time, you'll be able to deal with more easily and with more passion. You will find life more interesting and rewarding when you don't take yourself or the things around you quite so seriously.

****

The two characters in *Finding Your Soul At Work At Home, and When You're Alone!* are William, a 37 year-old midlevel manager in a large corporation located in the city. He is struggling with his life. Charmaine is a wise older woman who becomes William's mentor.

In this story, Charmaine helps William discover the Eight Clues that nobody ever taught him. First she helps William understand the mechanics of how we are 'wired up' and then practical ways to effectively use those tools in his daily life. This story is about William's quest to find his soul.

The Eight Clues

Clue # 1: *Suffering is a Gift in Disguise.*

All suffering, whether it is physical, emotional or spiritual is an exquisitely designed, divinely inspired and perfectly functioning communication system. Suffering is a gift. It is mind, body and spirit working together to tell us something we need to know to help us heal ourselves. Our pain and suffering only exist to serve us. So go toward it. Explore it. Discover what it is there to tell you. *Opening your heart to your suffering is the pathway to your freedom from it.*

Clue #2: *Live Your Life in Each Moment of Now.*

Being present and living in the moment is being totally absorbed and involved with all of your senses in the present. It's not living in the past nor is it imagining the uncertainties of the future. Living in moments of now frees you from judging, comparing, labeling and assigning credit or blame. *Being totally present and living in the moment relieves fear, worry, anxiety and life stress.*

Clue #3: *Learn to Choose Soul Over Ego, Love Over Fear.*

We can learn to choose our soul rather than ego, love over fear, an open heart over a closed one, our 'big mind' over our 'little mind'. Which one you live your life from in each moment is ultimately what determines the quality of your life. The soul is your access point to the Source and all its gifts. The value of the ego is that it is the predetermined mechanism by which the Source creates the unique and inescapable opportunities for each of us to exercise our free will to do the growing and expanding work we came here to do. *Understanding and consciously participating in the dance between the soul and ego and learning to choose between them is the key to living effectively, with passion and wonder.*

Clue #4: *Practice Loving Yourself.*

Loving yourself is embracing who you really are. It is holding yourself with tenderness and mercy. It is having compassion for yourself. It is being patient with all your shortcomings and mistakes as well as with your strengths and successes. Loving yourself opens the possibility to love others. It gives us access to feeling a sense of connectedness with the earth, all the creatures and all of humanity. Loving yourself at this soulful level is not selfish or arrogant. *Loving yourself is what happens when the ego allows in the soul's divine love.*

Clue #5: Be Honest With Yourself in All Things.

The power of honesty is that the more you tell the truth to yourself and the world around you, the more you are aligned with your authentic self, your soul. Though we are all quite transparent, the reason for telling the truth is not so much for others as for our own benefit. With it comes a feeling of aliveness, authenticity and new life-energy. *All honesty begins with honesty with yourself.*

Clue #6: Let Go of Attachment to Outcome.

Forming attachments is the source of all suffering. When you learn to practice letting go of attachment, you will discover that the sense of peace and joy you seek out in the world actually comes from and through your deeper self. Attachments include our addictions to people, activities, substances and beliefs. *Attachment to unchallenged patterns of thinking is an almost universal cause of great suffering.*

Clue #7: Forgiveness is a Gift that Transforms the Giver.

Develop both your inclination and your ability to forgive yourself and others. Unforgiveness is a form of attachment that can cause great suffering. Like spite and revenge, it is a poison that will affect not only your thinking but your body. *Learning to forgive can free you from guilt and resentment.*

Clue #8: Practice Some Form of Meditation.

Meditation is the single most powerful practice that can help free ourselves from fear and suffering. All suffering comes from the ego forming attachments. All attachments are formed by thoughts. Meditation is the moment-to-moment practice of letting go of the attachments formed by those thoughts. Meditation can take many forms. Find what works best for you. It simply works. We can only do it or not do it. We can't even do it wrong. *Ultimately, the purpose of meditation is to help us identify with our soul rather than with our ego.*

Chapter Two

Looking for the Answers

William considered himself to be a regular guy. He was intelligent and hard working. He was very sensitive to the people and situations around him. People used to tell him what a great smile he had but now it felt forced. And he had this funny habit of tilting his head to the right when he was listening intently to someone. He knew how to be a good listener but he just didn't seem to be as interested in what others were saying any more.

William knew that women seemed to be attracted to him but he never really knew why. He was generally well groomed but recently he had let his appearance slip. He stopped shining his shoes. He was not as concerned about his clothes as he used to be. He didn't bother to shave every day. He recalled how he used to enjoy getting a facial occasionally, not something he generally shared with his buddies. But in the last few months, he didn't seem to care as much about how he looked or doing the kinds of things that made him feel good.

William was not what you would call a theater buff but he did enjoy going to plays and musicals from time to time, especially with his old friends. He remembered how they would then go out for a fine meal together. He liked good food and was always appreciative of good service. He realized he hadn't been out like that in a very long time. In fact he had isolated himself and was not doing much of anything he had enjoyed in the past.

People had always enjoyed his wry sense of humor but lately it had turned pretty caustic. He used to enjoy reading about history and current events, reading several newspapers every day. But in the last year or so William had become fairly cynical about world and national politics. In fact, he recently had found himself getting angry at all the negative stories on the local evening news. It was just one gruesome report after another about his community and his neighbors being in some kind of crisis. It was all too depressing. He decided to stop watching the late night news.

William had an old friend named Bob who would call him once in a while. Lately, William felt so miserable and uninteresting that he would avoid Bob's calls. He'd just let the answering machine pick it up. It's funny, Bob would always make some positive statement like "I miss you bud" or "Let's get together and have some laughs - I miss your sense of humor". William stopped returning the calls, afraid that Bob would see what a 'downer' he was and how boring he had become.

He made decent money and had a reasonably nice place to live. He had come to this city several years ago for what looked like an excellent career move. But it hadn't quite worked out that way. William was generally unhappy. In fact, he was downright miserable.

One Friday evening, after coming home from work the same old way he always came home from work, he began to realize just how sad he really was. He knew he had been sad for a long time. But it was getting worse. He'd been trying to hold it together for many months now but he felt like he was losing his grip. He was having a hard time stuffing the feelings he'd been trying not to look at.

William didn't like his job. He knew many people at his company were unhappy too. It just wasn't a very friendly place to work. William was a supervisor and he knew he wasn't giving his people the kind of support and direction they needed. He never really felt in control of his group either.

There was a lot of friction with his boss, who was always on his back, complaining and pressuring to keep his staff producing more and more. He was angry at his boss for working him so many long hours and never giving him credit for the good work he had done. Yesterday his boss walked right past him and didn't even notice or acknowledge him. He felt invisible - like he wasn't worth anything to anybody.

It was no secret that some of the accounting people were being pressured to change some of the numbers to make things look better than they actually were. He knew there were lots of unethical practices going on at his company. But William didn't know what to do about it. He felt he had been deceived by the personnel manager that had hired him. He was angry about that and felt increasingly ashamed to be associated with this company.

Lately he'd been feeling really anxious at work. He was having trouble concentrating and making decisions. He also noticed he was starting to forget the simplest things. There was this nervous feeling like it was just a matter of time before he got caught, being a kid attempting a grown-up job. They would all see that he was not really qualified to be a supervisor.

In the last three weeks William had been having quite a few headaches and sometimes his heart raced. He'd feel all sweaty and thought he might fall over or go crazy or even die. At that moment the thought of dying almost seemed like a welcome relief.

William was a very lonely man. He had divorced several years ago, just before he came to this city. He didn't have a best friend. He hadn't had a best friend since high school. William realized he really didn't have any friends at all - not anybody he could really talk to. He was very isolated. Some of the other folks at work had parties from time to time. But they never invited him anymore. They used to invite him but he seldom felt comfortable enough to go. So they stopped asking.

William hadn't seen his parents or his brothers and sister in several years. He missed them a lot.

"Why haven't I stayed in touch with them?" he thought sadly. "I haven't called or visited them since I moved here. It's not because they haven't tried to stay in touch with me. They used to call regularly until I stopped returning their phone calls and e-mails. I really miss talking to my mom. She just seemed to love me no matter what. I always felt safe with her." In that moment William felt very much alone.

It seemed that nobody really knew how he felt. In fact, he wasn't sure he even knew how he felt. He'd worked pretty hard for a long time to avoid letting his feelings come to the surface. "A guy should be strong - stay in control of his feelings, right?" But it wasn't working anymore.

William had never really thought much about what he was feeling and he sure hadn't ever talked about it! He wondered if that had something to do with his divorce. His former wife often complained that he never talked to her - never really let her in on his true feelings. But how could he? Sometimes he felt scared and so unsure of himself. He couldn't let her know he felt that kind of stuff. Could he?

That evening, sitting alone on a bench at the park near where he lived, William pondered these things. He remembered that his father and one of his uncles used to complain about similar feelings. Was it genetic? Had he inherited a bad attitude and negative feelings from his family? His mom and sister weren't like that. It was all too confusing. Well, whatever the case, he had a lot of good reasons to feel badly.

Lately, William hadn't been taking very good care of himself, either. He had developed an unhealthy relationship with food - an increasing variety of junk food - and way too much of it!

"I know sometimes I eat to comfort myself. It's like trying to fill a void," he muttered desolately, popping another mouthful of french fries. "But the more I stuff it in, the bigger the void becomes. There's no filling the emptiness!"

The commute to work on the jam-packed freeway made him tense and anxious. The only exercise he ever got anymore was walking the two blocks from where he parked his car to his high-rise office building.

"That two block walk to work feels like all the exercise I can handle," William told himself. Yet he noticed his weight was up a little over 200 pounds. In college he had been a trim 175.

"How'd that happen?" he asked himself sarcastically, as he continued to scarf down his dinner - a double-bacon cheese burger, fries and a chocolate shake.

To make matters worse, William felt tired most of the time. He'd been having a hard time getting to sleep lately. He often woke in the middle of the night, worried about money, his job, his thinning hair ...... tossing and turning for hours.

Some nights, William wallowed for hours in angry fantasies about his boss and his company's insensitive and unethical practices. He felt guilty and ashamed to be part of a company that seemed to be only motivated by greed. Then he'd have difficulty getting back to sleep. No wonder he never felt rested in the mornings anymore.

"I can't remember the last time I slept through the night," he moaned. "What I'd give for just one good night's sleep!"

William had been doing other things he knew probably weren't good for him. Like spending too much time down at the local pub, drinking a little more beer than was good for him. He'd started to drink at home when he was alone, too. The alcohol's numbing effect only gave him temporary relief from his clamoring emotions. And he watched too much television - sometimes looking at pornography on the Internet. William was one lonely guy. And scared.

"I know I'm in trouble but what do I do about it," he wondered, gazing at his reflection in a puddle of water under his feet by the bench. That's when he noticed bags under his eyes. "My skin doesn't look that great either."

"Well, you'll just have to put on a good face, stay in control and keep going," he advised the reflection with macho bravado. "That's what men are expected to do. The way to survive in this corporate world is to stay in control and just keep going. Keep putting one slow-moving foot in front of the other. Day after day," he concluded morosely.

"What's my alternative," he asked, wishing the man reflected in the puddle could suggest one. Lately, William had been working overtime trying to keep it together. And there just never seemed to be enough time or money. He'd been trying his best to avoid his pain but it just wasn't working anymore.

William didn't really have any hobbies or outside interests any more. He realized he hadn't done any of the things he used to enjoy as a kid, like get together with his buddies and kick the soccer ball around.

"I haven't shot hoops or ridden my bike in years," William sighed. "Man, that used to be fun."

"I haven't gone dancing, either," he exclaimed. "Not since I left home. I used to feel so alive on the dance floor." He smiled at the memory. "Everybody said I had natural rhythm." He also remembered with pleasure singing as a carefree young man while standing in long hot showers.

"...and I haven't sung a note in ages!"

"I used to be pretty good at baseball when I was young," William pointed out to his reflected image in the puddle. "Hey! I'm not that old," he objected. "I just *feel* old - and tired. I know lots of people who still play softball and soccer! Why haven't I felt like joining them? I guess I don't have passion for much of anything in my life anymore," William said flatly.

William didn't know if he believed in God or not. In fact, he didn't have a strong belief in anything bigger than himself. He hadn't been to church in years - couldn't agree with everything any one church taught. Much of what they had to say simply didn't make sense to his logical mind. So he just didn't go.

But he remembered when he was younger, there was something special about being in church with his family. He seemed to feel better when he went where other people gathered to celebrate life. He enjoyed the singing, and he did kind of like dressing up in his tweed jacket and string tie. "And the mountains of fresh-baked cookies after the service," William recalled fondly, "were homemade heaven!"

But that is not the way it felt now. He was depressed and it narrowed his world. "I feel like I've become so self-absorbed that hope in the future and any real connection with other people has disappeared. I have lost faith and a belief that there is any good in the universe." He felt heavy all over. "I seem to have gotten fixated on the how hostile and uncaring the world seems. Everything dies. Everything is just so transient." He paused to rub the tightness in his neck. "Why bother to care about anything? It would only hurt more to care." William wondered if he'd ever be happy again. He felt hopeless and helpless to do anything about it. He didn't see that there was anything he could do that would make him feel better.

As he sat alone on the bench, all the rest of the feelings he'd been stuffing came to the surface and washed over him: depression, anxiety, sadness, loneliness, fear, confusion and shame. He felt intense frustration with everybody lately, including himself. He realized how angry he'd been getting at all the jerks on the crowded freeway on his way to work each morning. "I guess maybe I've become one of them."

William slowly walked home. When he got there he threw his coat on the couch and noticed how messy the place was. His windows were dirty, too.

"No wonder I have such a bad *outlook*," he snickered inwardly. "Look at this pig sty. You'd think 50 frat boys had just thrown a kegger party in here. No wonder my life feels like such a mess." William suddenly realized that he hadn't laughed in a long, long time.

He also noticed that the mirror in the bathroom was smudgy and the laundry wasn't done. There were still dishes in the sink from last week. And not much that could be classified as edible was in the refrigerator, either. He realized he hadn't had anybody over to his place as long as he'd been there. Looking around, he knew he'd feel embarrassed to entertain guests. William felt ashamed - a fairly common feeling lately.

It began to dawn on him that beneath his tangle of feelings was a deeply rooted, old thought that if people really knew him - what he felt and what he thought, who he really was - they wouldn't like him. They wouldn't want to have anything to do with him.

"No wonder I've isolated myself! I'm afraid to let anybody see who I've become."

Now William felt even more hopeless. And he didn't have any idea what to do about it!

He thought about others he knew and didn't think any of them seemed really happy either.

"Well, nobody except maybe my old friend Bob or my neighbor George," William admitted to himself. "George always seems to be happy."

George always had a friendly 'hello' for William when he saw him in the neighborhood. William never had stopped to talk to George, though. Being so stressed from work, he'd just nod, lower his sad eyes and haul his weary self home.

"George always seems to have a good time hanging out with family and friends," sighed William. "He's a lucky man. I sure wish I had a life like George's!"

William wondered if *how* he was thinking about things could be part of his problem. He sensed that *how he thought* probably had a direct relationship to *how he felt*. But he just couldn't see any way to change how he thought.

William had a lot of good reasons to feel bad so he suspected his thinking couldn't be all of the problem. But trying to figure it out was too complicated. He felt confused, numb and powerless

Late that night William walked up the hill from his house, to where the bridge overlooked the city. The night was very clear and the full moon shone brightly. It was a wonderful place to look out over the vast expanse of lights which was now his world. He looked out in the direction of the city where he had left his family and friends - his old home. Sometimes William thought about jumping off the bridge.

"I don't really want to... but sometimes life just seems harder than dying. I'm so tired of the pain and suffering and the emptiness that fills my life. At this point in my life it feels like I have to face the reality that my childhood dreams simply haven't come true. But I don't want to give up on me. I just don't know what to do. I haven't got a clue."

"A long, long time ago when I was a little kid, I had a really clear feeling there was a reason I was alive. I remember back when I instinctively knew there was something I was supposed to do or be. Though I didn't know what that purpose was, I knew it was true! That feeling isn't quite so clear anymore."

William stood by the rail of the bridge looking out at the miles and miles of concrete jungle below him. He felt more sad and lonely and hopeless than he had ever let himself feel. William began to cry. He couldn't stop himself this time.

He cried deep and he cried hard and he cried long. He sobbed like a scared, lonely child. He let himself cry like he had never let himself cry before.

He cried about the end of his marriage.

"Why couldn't I make it work? She was such a sweetheart, too."

He cried about his life not turning out the way he had hoped it would.

"What happened?" he wailed.

The tears rolled down his sallow cheeks as all his heartache washed over him. He felt like an emotional basket case but right then he didn't care. William just let it happen.

William cried about his hopeless situation at work. He cried about not having anything in his life to look forward to - no activities, no real friends and nobody to touch him or to lovingly touch. He cried and cried and cried.

After a while the crying stopped. He didn't know how long he'd been standing there or how much time had passed. But he noticed that some of the most painful feelings had passed too. William realized that for the first time in a long time he didn't feel quite so miserable.

"Whew," he thought. "What a relief! Letting myself cry actually helped me feel better. How could that be? This is all so confusing. Oh, well, I'm tired... think I'll go home and go to bed."

He slept through the entire night and awoke feeling rested. William had just had the best night's sleep he could remember in months.

"Go figure," he exclaimed. "I think I'll eat a nice big breakfast and then do the dishes and clean this place up a bit!"

While William vacuumed, he grinned boyishly and cracked a joke.

"Life sucks!" Once, he had liked his sense of humor. Where had it been for so long?

"Why is it so hard - and scary - to allow myself to feel all those emotions he wondered.

Later he caught himself whistling as he picked up an old sock from behind the couch.

"I know I need help but I don't know where to turn," he said to the dead fern he had forgotten to water. "There must be somebody I could I trust with all my stuff.

Chapter Three

Clue # 1

Suffering is a Gift in Disguise

William walked in his neighborhood on a warm Saturday afternoon as he searched for some escape from his misery. He started thinking about all the pain and sadness he'd been feeling. He was suffering and generally miserable. He wanted to run away from the pain. Recently he'd been getting sudden feelings of fear that struck repeatedly and without warning. He often felt he would pass out at any second, feeling dizzy with some trouble breathing. He'd been feeling more confused, unable to focus and had been having difficulties making decisions. And he was frequently overwhelmed by feelings of hopelessness. There seemed to be no way out. He thought about how angry he was at his boss for working him so hard and never giving him credit for his good work. He felt uncomfortable about his job and the company he worked for.

Walking along a jogger's path at the park near where he lived, William followed a gently flowing creek and soon entered a clearing deep in the park. He discovered the amazing waterfall his friend George had told him about. It must have been fifty feet high. The water cascaded into a magnificent lagoon. He slowly walked over and stood by the water's edge, just basking in the peaceful beauty. After a while, William took off his shoes and socks and soaked his tired feet in the warm shallows.

"Funny," he muttered thoughtfully. "Just a moment before, I was feeling bad but right now it feels like I might just make it through another day!"

"Hello," said a soft voice that sounded very near.

William looked around but didn't see anybody. "Now I'm hearing voices! Am I going crazy?" he wondered.

Then he saw a strikingly lovely woman with long flowing silver hair sitting comfortably atop a large boulder near him. Her gentle features were accented by clear, intuitive green eyes.

"My name is Charmaine," she said, inviting conversation.

William was startled but curious why this mysterious woman would speak to him, a stranger. She was friendly and seemed very peaceful and calm.

"Hi. I'm William. Do you live around here?"

"No, not really," said Charmaine. "But I come here to meditate sometimes."

"Meditate?"

"It's how I find peacefulness and clarity." Sensing his pain, she said, "It's a way to relax and deal with stress. And to re-energize."

" I could use some of that," William sighed. "I've really been struggling lately."

William didn't know why he had just said that. It was not at all like him to be so open with a stranger. He felt a little embarrassed. Skillfully changing the subject, he said, "So, what do you do for a living?"

"I'm into metaphysical electronics."

"Metaphysical electronics?"

"I spend most of my time helping folks understand how their life experience is 'wired up'. I help them discover how their minds, bodies and hearts determine the way they feel from moment to moment," said Charmaine. "I help them discover the Eight Clues to living a happy, effective and more satisfying life."

"Where did you learn about these Clues?"

"Actually, I first learned them from a wise, old gentleman a long time ago. I also learned by simply paying attention to my own life experiences."

"Do you think the Eight Clues could help me?"

Charmaine smiled. "I'm pretty sure they could."

"I've been unhappy for quite awhile."

"Can you be more specific and name some of your feelings?"

"I've never let myself get too specific about them. It's bad enough to feel stuck in this misery and on top of that I guess I feel ashamed for even having all these bad feelings. I don't really know what to do with feelings except to try to stay in control of them. To answer your question, I guess I've been angry, sad, lonely and more than a little confused."

"Perhaps you just don't understand the importance of being aware of, and paying attention to your feelings - all of them. Our feelings exist to serve us, you know. They can actually guide us in living a happier and more effective life. The first of the Eight Clues is to understand the *gift of suffering*."

"The ...*gift* ...of suffering? Suffering doesn't feel like a gift," William exclaimed. "It hurts! Suffering pretty much ruins every moment of my life. How can suffering be a gift?"

Charmaine smiled again as she rubbed her own sore ankle.

"Suffering is a gift in disguise," she explained. "All suffering, whether it is physical, emotional or spiritual, is an exquisitely designed, divinely inspired and perfectly functioning communication system."

"That's a mouthful," said William, grinning.

"It's our mind, body and spirit working together to give us the information we need to help us heal ourselves. So, you see, pain is a necessary and normal part of our lives."

"Our job," she said, "is not to 'stuff' or avoid the feelings we *think* are bad. Neither is it to numb ourselves to them or ignore them. Every feeling has a value and a purpose. They are all meant to serve us. We can learn to go *toward* our feelings - explore them - in order to discover what that particular experience of joy or suffering is trying to tell us."

"What do you mean, 'go toward our feelings'?"

"To go toward your feelings is to *allow* yourself to feel them. That's how we process feelings – to move *through* them, not around them. That's how we *learn* from our feelings rather than getting *stuck* in them."

"Hmm."

"If you put your finger on a hot stove, the pain is not the problem. The problem is that your finger is on a hot stove. The pain you feel tells you exactly what to do to stop the suffering. It isn't telling you to leave it there and cry louder - or to scratch your left ear. It's telling you to take your finger off the hot stove."

"That makes sense."

"And notice that when you burn your finger, you get a little blister, a healing reminder. But your arm doesn't fall off. What I mean is that the Universe is not out to get you. It will only give you the amount of suffering you need in order to learn whatever it is there to tell you."

"Feedback," William nodded, beginning to get the picture.

"Exactly. The blister is a reminder that your finger is beginning to heal from the painful event, from the inside out. And that's how suffering works too. If you are *willing* to face your suffering you'll soon see signs of healing."

"But expecting someone who's in pain to just 'face his suffering' sounds a little hardhearted," objected William.

"On the surface it may sound that way. But if you resist, that is, stuff and ignore your suffering, it will only get worse. That's a fairly accurate indicator that you have not suffered enough yet. Sooner or later, when the suffering gets uncomfortable enough, you'll be forced by your very symptoms to face the thing you are afraid to face. It's totally up to each of us how much and how long we suffer. Consider your suffering as a light guiding you on the pathway to your freedom from it."

"But how does that relate to my everyday life? What does it have to do with my job, for instance?"

"If you are suffering at work," Charmaine said, "one of two things is generally the problem. Either you have not learned to do your job in a way that nurtures your soul, or you are in the wrong job. The test is whether it makes you feel good, fulfilled, satisfied, and energized. Do you feel like you are making a worthwhile and valued contribution? If not, you may be in the wrong job. Or you may be with a company that you cannot totally support and feel good about. It's usually the first of these two problems - but not always. Sometimes it's a combination of the two. You can tell if your work nurtures your soul because you will feel energized by it. You'll use your strengths and talents in a way that benefits both you and your employer."

"What if it's the wrong job but you need the money?"

"It's simply a matter of how much you are willing to suffer for the money. Some jobs can be so toxic - so unhealthy and uncomfortable - that you can not have them in your life in a way that nurtures your soul. It's the same with any relationship, activity or even a substance that brings you down. They become what I call 'soul robbing activities'. Ultimately, you must move away from them."

"Easier said than done!" said William.

"Usually it's a matter of finding a way to have that job in your life so that it *does* nurture your soul. It's true about any activity, relationship or substance in your life. It may require a shift in how you are thinking about it. After all, your thoughts are the source of your uncomfortable feelings. You may need to focus on the aspects of your job that make you feel most validated and find most energizing," Charmaine said. "Focus on your strengths, on the places where you find real meaning and value in your work. If you are still suffering, then pay attention to what those feelings are trying to tell you. If there is something you need to change, then change it. Your suffering will tell you exactly where to look for the answer. You just have to be willing to go toward the feelings, be honest with yourself and keep your heart open."

"How?"

"Try letting go of any self-criticism or resistance to what you see and feel about yourself and others or the situation you're in. Remember, your feelings - all of them - were designed to serve you."

"The other night", said William, hoping Charmaine wouldn't think he was a wimp, "I was feeling angry and lonely and definitely at the end of my rope. I .... started to cry. I couldn't stop no matter how hard I tried, and all these feelings just came pouring out of me. So I finally just let it happen. The weird thing is after I cried for a while, I felt better. How could letting myself feel bad feel so good?"

"Ah," said Charmaine, "now you are getting to the heart of the matter. You came to a point where you had finally suffered enough. You simply couldn't stuff the feelings that kept coming up anymore. And that's a good thing. It was a *relief to release*, like an emotional safety valve. Your feelings are not the enemy, William. They are part of your internal communications system."

"You might think of feelings as *emotional gas*, she said. "They are real. They come from deep inside and they need to come out. In fact, if you don't find some way to express them they will find their own way out. They'll begin to seep out of you at the most inappropriate times and places, everywhere in your life. They will begin to create symptoms in your body such as lower back pain, headaches, dizziness, heartburn and stomach aches. You may also find yourself feeling confused and having difficulty deciding even the most simple things. You'll see symptoms in your relationships as well, such as guilt, resentment or jealousy. You'll find them showing up in your work, as anger, apathy, anxiety or fear, for example. You'll find yourself being overly critical of yourself and others at home and on the job. "

"Emotional gas," mused William. I like that analogy. That's exactly how I've been feeling. Have I had some serious gas!" William grinned sarcastically.

Charmaine laughed. "All our emotions are of value and serve a purpose, William. We're not even capable of unacceptable feelings, only unacceptable behaviors. Have you ever had a really good feeling?"

"Sure. It felt great to put my feet in the lagoon and look at the waterfall."

"Those feelings are also there to tell you something you need to know."

"So all of our feelings really are useful indicators."

"You bet! And here's another interesting aspect to the gift of suffering. Have you ever had a really good feeling and tried to hold onto it?"

"Oh, yes! But it always goes away."

"That's true," Charmaine said. "You can't hold onto a really good feeling no matter how hard you try. But that's not only true of good feelings. It's true of *all* feelings. If you have a really bad feeling and you allow yourself to feel it, try to feel it - and even try to hold onto it and make it more intense - you will feel it. And then it will simply disappear. It's only our fear of a feeling, our resistance and objection to it, that can keep us stuck in it. It's also our resistance and objection to the facts and circumstances that we think caused our feelings that can keep us stuck in it. Resistance *causes* persistence."

"Ok," said William, "let me say this back to you to see if I get what you're saying. If I stuff my uncomfortable feelings, they stay inside, poisoning me. But if I *feel* my feelings, or go toward them, they dissipate!"

"Yes! This is all very simple at one level. But it's not necessarily *easy* to do. I've been practicing going toward my feelings for a long time and I can't always do it."

"Why not?"

"Sometimes I've just not suffered enough yet."

"Whoa! Are you into masochism? Because if you are..."

"No," Charmaine chuckled. "But I'm reminded of a bright young woman I once knew named Lisa. She complained about some of the same kind of things that you mentioned about your job. When she started she was enthusiastic and very positive. In time, the company pressured her to work longer and longer hours with less and less support, acknowledgment and appreciation. She didn't feel valued or respected for her efforts. When she went home at night she began to notice that she was angry and impatient with her husband and kids. She started getting migraines and no longer felt she had time to take care of herself. She gained weight and began losing contact with some of the friends she used to exercise with."

"Oh, I can relate to that! So, what did she do then?"

"She left. She lived within walking distance to work and was well-paid but it finally got to a point that the pain and suffering she felt in her job, finally became greater than the benefits. It's what I call doing an 'emotional-cost-benefit analysis'. Like many of us, Lisa was very tenacious, which can be a good thing. The other side of tenacity is that sometimes it can be difficult to know when and how to let go of a bad situation."

"Have you ever noticed how we tend to repeat our mistakes over and over again? We keep running into the same kind of problems in life, bringing up in us the same unpleasant feelings, over and over again. Perhaps we feel put down, made wrong, ignored. The pattern repeats itself at home, at work, on the freeway, in the grocery store and in our personal relationships. And we think the problem is out there. Think of it this way. By our very nature we attract, like a magnet, the very situations and people we need. We do this in order to create for ourselves an 'inescapable opportunity' to face the next thing we are ready to learn. The Universe is impeccable in its ability to provide us as many opportunities as we need to learn whatever that particular suffering is there to teach us. So we usually don't get to experience the lesson and the suffering just once. Even after we think we may have learned a lesson, the Universe will continue to give us opportunities to show that we 'get it'. And it will continue to show up until the issue simply begins to slowly disappear in our life. And even then it will occasionally show up just as a little reminder."

"Suffering is truly a gift in disguise," Charmaine continued.

"Understanding the value of suffering can lead to a happier and more productive life."

"A gift in disguise," William repeated hopefully. "I want to hear more about this because suffering is one thing I have plenty of!"

"So William, tell me first, why did you come to this waterfall?"

"When I was a lot younger, a couple of my buddies and I used to stand under a waterfall laughing and horsing around," William sighed happily at the memory. "So I thought just coming here and looking at it might help me feel better."

"Let's go stand by the waterfall right now."

"Nah, I am a full-grown man. I don't do things like that anymore. Besides, you'll get that clothes wet if you get too close to it."

Charmaine laughed. "I can stand close to the waterfall with you and still be reasonably dry. Come on, I'll show you." Charmaine reached into her large white backpack, pulled out a colorful parasol and began singing an old blues song that seemed to come from deep within her soul.

William smiled at Charmaine rhythmically moving to her own music. He thought, 'Why not?' and happily joined her beside the waterfall. The cool mist rising from it felt soothing on his warm body. A broad, boyish smile spreading across his face, William broke exuberantly into a stanza of *Jungle Boogie*. Charmaine stood beside him with droplets bouncing off her parasol and joined in with a bass harmony line. Well, it wasn't very bass. But it had soul!

William let the mist from the crystal clear water wash over him, swaying to the rhythm of their song. They stayed by the waterfall, luxuriating in its coolness for quite a while. Then they strolled to other side of the lagoon.

"Come on, William. I'll race you over to that water tower at the edge of the park!"

"Well, that's not really fair to you," William laughed. "I'm younger and faster than you!"

"Oh, yes it is." Charmaine said as she pulled out a pair of roller blades from her backpack and quickly fastened them."

They both laughed. William grunted and groaned as he playfully bounded toward the tower. Charmaine rolled effortlessly along the paved path with a radiant smile on her ageless face.

"Oo-eee!" Charmaine whooped as she reached the mark well ahead of William. He plopped down on the grass by the tower and she sat beside him quietly basking in the sun while William caught his breath.

"This feels great," sighed William. "Why can't I feel like this all the time?"

"You can feel like this more of the time than you might imagine," Charmaine said. "But suffering is a natural part of life, William. We suffer because we get attached to an outcome, to the idea that we'd be happy if only we had more money or just the right job or the perfect mate. And, of course, that isn't true in the long run. Suffering happens when we get caught up in the past or the future and lose our sense of being fully present. Sometimes suffering rises from our need to be right, from our need to be special or from cherishing ourselves over others. We suffer when we hold on to our need to assign blame - or even credit. We suffer as a result of constantly wanting and craving. We suffer when we compare, judge and criticize ourselves and others. These are only some of the many ways we create our own suffering because we think our happiness depends on things being a certain way 'out in the world'."

"Wow, that's a lot to wrap my mind around..."

"Wrapping our mind around life's events is exactly the problem," she said. "It is the source of our suffering. It really is *all* in our head, an illusion!"

"Are you trying to tell me that all my problems are in my head?"

"Yes, that's exactly what I'm telling you, William. Where else do you think they could come from? It is our mind's *thoughts* that *cause our experiences,* not the events themselves. For right now, just remember that much of our pain is really 'anticipatory suffering'," Charmaine said.

"...and a lot to wrap my *tongue* around! What's anticipatory suffering, anyhow?"

"Expecting suffering that hasn't even happened yet - and probably won't," she said. "It's fed by our memories and beliefs from past conditioning and experiences we resisted. Remember William, our real pain and suffering doesn't actually come from the facts and events in our life. It comes from our *objection* to and our *resistance* to those facts and events."

"Hmmm," said William. "That's a whole different way to look at it."

"It's the *meaning we add* to the facts and events that causes our grief. And those meanings we add are often not based in reality. They generally come from unseen and long-held attitudes, beliefs and assumptions we make about the things that happen in our world. It's helpful to ask ourselves whether or not these thoughts continue to serve us."

"Now, I can understand that," William exclaimed. "I'm one hurtin' guy!"

"Some of our worst experiences of suffering actually come from resistance to our pain. Suffering, when resisted, can really hurt. But suffering, when embraced, is quite different."

"Do you remember when you were hurting so badly the other night?"

"Sure. How can I forget?"

"Wasn't the pain most intense when you fought against experiencing your feelings?"

"Yes, I guess so!"

"But did you notice what happened when you finally surrendered and let it happen?"

"Ummm... it still hurt... but now I'd say that it hurt... just right!"

"That's what I call 'exquisite pain'," Charmaine said. "It's suffering unresisted. It's real. It's deep. And it feels really good to just let it happen."

"You're right, it does feel better than stuffing it until you hurt."

"Stuffing it just extends and deepens the suffering, doesn't it? Remember pain is designed to serve you. So when you become aware of pain and go toward it, you actually take a short cut to your freedom from it. Look for what the suffering is trying to tell you. It is trying to tell you that what you are doing is not going to give you what you want. Then you can use the energy that would have been expended 'keeping a lid on it' for something more fun."

"I'm for that!"

"You know, your mind and body are one."

"I'm not sure I get what you mean by that."

"Nothing happens to us physically that doesn't effect us emotionally. On the other hand, nothing can happen to us emotionally that doesn't effect us physically. We used to think that which we call our 'mind' was in our brain. Now we know that our 'mind' is in every cell of our body. So whenever we suffer emotionally, it will reveal a symptom somewhere in our body. For example, when you are angry at your boss, where in your body do you feel it?"

"I don't know."

"Think about a moment when you were really upset with him."

"Well, I remember the time I did an incredible job on the Spencer account and my boss never recognized any of my efforts."

"What do you notice in your body right now?"

After a few moments William said, "My jaw is tight."

"Now think about missing your family and friends back home. Where do you feel that?"

William slumped forward. His shoulders got heavy. His breath shortened and he stared at the ground. He thought for a long moment. "I feel it deep in my chest."

Charmaine saw a tear in William's eye. "I'm sorry you're hurting so much. I know what it feels like to miss having loved ones close by. But if you pay attention to all your feelings, you'll begin to recognize what feels good and what doesn't. Then you'll understand what you must do to create more peace and happiness in your life."

"Charmaine," William protested. "I've been struggling to stay in control of my feelings all my life! I thought that's what we're supposed to do, especially us guys."

"You're right. Most of us, especially 'you guys', have been taught that. You think it is essential to stay in control."

"Why does the thought of showing my feelings seem so scary?"

"It's because we think our survival literally depends on staying in control. Our best strategy for staying in control is to avoid intense feelings because when we are experiencing those intense feelings we are not in control. That's why we call them feelings. And one of our mind's favorite strategies for avoiding feelings is to try to figure out *why* we are feeling them. Our mind thinks that if we could just figure out *why* we are feeling them, then we would not actually have to feel them, thereby losing our illusory experience of being in control."

"Well, sometimes it sure seems like I know why I'm feeling certain emotions, especially when it's the things that make me 'mad in the face'," William exclaimed with a silly grin.

"But the facts and circumstances of our world do not *cause* our feelings, William," she replied. "They *trigger* them. The feelings originate within us. As a dear and very wise old gray haired mentor of mine named John Enright once told me, 'The world is just out there *worlding*. Whatever we experience is what we bring to it."

"I get it. Circumstances are neutral!"

"Exactly. What we experience is what we bring to the party. Our thoughts are the horse that our feelings ride in on. Sometimes we just do too much thinking and not enough feeling. It's natural for us to have feelings. It's just much more effective to pay attention to what we're feeling rather than why we are feeling it. Feeling the feelings without adding *meaning* is generally the shortest route *through* them."

"Oh, okay. That makes sense."

"The irony is that once you move through the feelings without objection or resistance and without adding additional meaning to them, you are much more likely to have an 'ah-ha' moment! You have a much clearer sense of what they are trying to tell you and what, if anything, you need to do about them. And then, of course, things change."

"So just when I've got things figured out things change!" William protested. "And I'm back to square one."

"That's the nature of the beast," Charmaine explained. "Life is a constant series of changes. If you begin to go toward the changes rather than fighting them, and they're *bound* to happen, you will be pleasantly surprised."

"By what?"

"By personal breakthroughs, creative thinking, more clarity and more effectiveness in everything you do. Your intuition and natural wisdom become available to you again. They get you in touch with your compassion, not only for yourself but for the suffering of others, including those that you feel may have wronged you. You begin to rediscover where your passions and interests lie. Lots of people rediscover their ability to be present and available in the moment and so, less fearful of intimacy and close relationships. It's all good stuff, William."

They sat quietly for awhile. Then William slowly got up and stretched out his arms with a big sigh.

"How do you feel right now, William?" asked Charmaine with a smile.

"I feel great!"

"And how do you feel *now*? Take a fresh look, William."

He thought about it for a moment. "I feel content. How could I feel so miserable one minute and so content the next?"

"Because each *moment of now* is a totally fresh possibility to be in your soul or in your ego. Just think! A new beginning each moment!"

"What do you mean by a 'moment of now'?"

"Let's walk and we can talk about that."

"Charmaine, would you like to see my favorite spot in the park?"

"I'd love to."

Summary

Clue # 1: Suffering is a Gift in Disguise.

All suffering, whether it is physical, emotional or spiritual is an exquisitely designed, divinely inspired and perfectly functioning communication system. Suffering is a gift. It is mind, body and spirit working together to tell us something we need to know to help us heal ourselves. Our pain and suffering only exist to serve us. So go toward it. Explore it. Discover what it is there to tell you. Opening your heart to your suffering is the pathway to your freedom from it.

- Our job is to go toward our feelings, explore them and discover what they are trying to tell us.

- Suffering is a natural part of life when we identify with our mind/body – our ego – rather than our soul.

- Suffering occurs when we form attachment in the world.

- Our real pain and suffering doesn't come from the facts and events in our life. It comes from our objecting and resisting those facts and events.

- Much of our pain is really anticipatory suffering.

- The Universe will only give you the amount of suffering you need in order to learn whatever it is there to tell you.

- Face the suffering and soon you will see signs of healing.

- If you resist, stuff and ignore the suffering, it will get worse.

- Experiencing your feelings without adding *meaning* is generally the shortest route *through* them.

- Pay attention to *what* you are feeling rather than *why* you are feeling it.

- Resistance to suffering causes the persistence of suffering.

- Use the 'emotional-cost-benefit' analysis.

- When we emotionally or spiritually suffer it will reveal a symptom somewhere in our body.

- Suffering is a light guiding you to your freedom from the suffering.

At Work

- Suffering at work means you are doing something that you cannot totally support and feel good about.

- Your work is nurturing your soul when you feel good, energized and are using your strengths and talents.

- If you have mercy and compassion for your own suffering it will be easier for you to have more understanding for others - including those who have wronged you.

The Benefits of Understanding Suffering

You will have more energy and less fear. You will move toward any changes you may need to make. You will have more breakthroughs, new creative thinking and more clarity. You will have more compassion for yourself and others. You will rediscover your passions and interests. You will be more present and less fearful of intimacy and closer relationships. You will be more effective in all things.

Exercise

"Resistance Causes Persistence"

This is a creative visualization exercise. We know that successful artists, musicians, athletes or business people quite frequently achieve amazing outcomes because they have imagined themselves accomplishing their goals before they've actually performed them. Your positive and creative thoughts can help you achieve whatever you want.

But this exercise is a here and now, internal process in which you visualize a place in your body where you are holding some pain or discomfort. It is a part of you from which you have fearfully separated yourself, a place where you are afraid to experience the physical and emotional feelings that are there.

Let go of any tendency to prematurely analyze or try to explain why you are feeling the sensation. Pay attention to what you are feeling rather than why you are feeling it. The feeling will tell you the why. Let your body rather than your mind tell you what you need to know.

This is an exercise to help you learn to see physical and emotional pain as a neutral sensation. If you think of the sensation as pain, that one thought automatically creates the feeling to be a negative and distancing relationship you have with that sensation, separate from yourself. This exercise will help you learn to see all your feelings as a natural and useful part of your life.

At first it may be useful to have someone slowly read this to you and guide you through it. Get in a comfortable position, sitting or lying down. Take a few easy breaths. Close your eyes.

Step 1: Scan your awareness and notice a negative emotion or a physical discomfort. The emotion might be sadness, jealousy, loneliness, boredom, anxiety or depression. The physical discomfort might be a chronic pain such as an old injury or illness. It could be a more short-lived discomfort such as an upset stomach or headache. Remember, since the mind and body are one, every emotional feeling will reveal itself somewhere in your body.

So now notice exactly where that feeling is in your body. (Pause)

Let yourself feel the full strength of that sensation in your body. (Pause)

On a scale from zero to ten, where zero is no awareness of any discomfort and ten is the worst pain you can imagine, give it a number. Assign a value to the pain or discomfort as it is right now, not where it was yesterday or where you are afraid it might be tomorrow.

Step 2: Gently focus all of your awareness and attention on that place in your body. Soften all around it. Invite the sensation to be there. See if you can make it bigger, more real and more intense. Stay totally present and focused on that area. (There is a part of you that may think this is counter intuitive, just the opposite of what you should do. The anticipation of going toward the feeling may seem scary or make you think you might die. But be assured it is safe. It actually can be very freeing to go toward and explore whatever physical sensation or emotion you are feeling.) (Pause)

Step 3: Imagine going inside of your own body and exploring where the sensation is. (Pause)

Invite that feeling to be there, exactly as it is, without any resistance or objection to it. Notice its precise location. (Pause)

Move all around it. *Lovingly* notice it. To *lovingly* notice you simply invite the sensation in with complete acceptance, with tenderness and compassion. Surrender to the feeling with a deep and natural sense of connection to it, free of any judgment, any sense of separation or rejection of the feeling. Now notice its shape and its size. (Pause)

Notice what color it is. (Pause)

Move closer to it. Imagine reaching out with your hand and gently touching it. Feel its texture. Notice if it's hot or cold, wet or dry, soft or hard. (Pause)

Notice anything you can about it. Curiously explore it - as a child would.

Know that the sensation is only there to serve you, to tell you something you need to know to help you heal yourself, to get your life back into balance physically, emotionally or spiritually.

Step 4: Now ask that part of your body a question about anything in your life. It might be about a troubled relationship, a concern about a child or parent, an unmet challenge in your education or career, a physical concern you know you have not taken care of, etc. Examples: "What are you trying to tell me?" "How long do I have to suffer?" "Why did she leave me?" "Could I lose my job?" (Pause)

Notice anything that comes into your awareness. Notice any thoughts, any flashes of memory or images that may come to you. Don't do anything with them. Just be the observer, a loving witness. (Pause)

Perhaps something comes up for you or perhaps nothing will. Sometimes the question you ask is the answer. (Pause)

Feel free to have a conversation with that sensation in your body. (Pause)

Take as much time as you like. Keep taking a fresh look. The feeling may shift or move or change in some way. It may remain unchanged. Contine to invite it to be there exactly as it is. Know that it is only there to serve you.

Step 5: With a deep sense of gratitude and appreciation for its commitment to serve you in exactly the way it is, imagine welcoming and embracing the physical sensation. (Pause)

Totally let go of any resistance or objection to its being there. Now imagine moving inside of it. (Pause)

Surrender to it. Let the feeling have you. (Pause)

Now imagine *becoming* it. (See yourself as the feeling itself. Identify with it rather than separate from it.) (Pause)

You may notice that as you let go of any tendency to distance yourself or separate yourself from the feeling, it begins to dissolve from your awareness.

Step 6: If the pain or discomfort is still there, or if it comes back into your awareness, simply go toward it again. Take a fresh look. Lovingly observe it; invite it to be there. Make it bigger, more real, more intense. Again, notice its exact location, its shape, its size and its texture. Ask it a question. Open yourself to whatever it is there to tell you. Have a conversation with it. Embrace it. Move inside of it. Let it have you. *Become* it. As you let go of all resistance and objection to it, letting go of any separation from it, the pain or discomfort will often begin to fade or completely disappear from your awareness.

Step 7: Notice on a scale of zero to ten how you experience that area of your body now. You may notice that the physical discomfort is now gone or has diminished slightly or dramatically. Use this process as often as you would like. With practice you will notice you can begin to do it very quickly. You will become more and more effective at applying this technique in many areas of your life.

Principle

Resistance causes persistence. This principle applies to all physical, emotional or spiritual suffering. As you let go of all resistance and objection to the painful feeling, letting go of the natural tendency to pull away, to separate yourself from the physical sensation, the physical or emotional pain will diminish or completely disappear from your awareness. This exercise can help remove the fear previously associated with pain so that it will have less power in your life.

The mind and body are one, not just metaphorically but quite literally. This is a powerful way to free yourself from much of your suffering. Remember, everything that affects you physically also affects you emotionally, and everything that affects you emotionally also affects you physically.

Chapter Four

Clue #2:

Live Your Life in Each Moment of Now.

As William and Charmaine moved through the park toward his favorite bench, he noticed that the park seemed alive with activity. William's heart was opening to the flow of life all around him. The colors seemed more vibrant, the scents more heady and the sounds —well, they were downright joyous to him! There was a mixed chorus of birds singing their sweet melodies. Couples held hands and laughed together. Children played happily. And for the first time in a very long time he felt like he had a new friend!

"Charmaine, you were going to tell me what you mean by a 'moment of now'?"

She walked ahead a short distance and stopped at William's favorite bench.

"Imagine your whole life is a movie, William," she began. "And imagine that each and every moment of your entire life, from the moment of your birth to this second, is stored on that roll of film. Now imagine that each *frame* of that film is one *moment of now*. There are millions, billions of them. Thinking of life and time in this linear way makes it easier for our mind to understand. Actually, it is a constant flow, like a river."

"Each frame of the movie is a moment of now?"

"It's a helpful image, isn't it? Being present in a moment of now is being aware of a single frame of that movie as it's happening. It's the awareness of the stream of our thoughts and physical sensations. It's being open to life. It's seeing with fresh eyes. It's listening to really hear rather than to plan what we will say or do next. It's being aware of all of our senses - touch, taste and smell, sound – wholly absorbed, totally present and completely involved. Being fully present in a moment of now is looking at everything as if you are seeing it for the first time. Remember when you were a child, in those wonderful moments when you felt curious, carefree, excited and safe?"

"Yeah."

"That's the quality of being fully present."

"I can see the benefit of being present in moments of now, Charmaine. I think some of my anxiety and not being fully in the moment happens when I'm worrying about what I'll say next. I feel a need to fill the air with talk. I think I've been afraid of silence. I think people will like me less if I'm not a good conversationalist. I don't think I've even been present with myself when I'm alone. Recently, most of my moments of now have been pretty discouraging - which usually haven't given me much hope for moments in the future."

"The key to living in each moment, William, is understanding that all we ever really have in this life is *right now*," she answered. "Oops, that moment is gone. Here comes another. There it goes. And now here is another one... "

"I can see that staying in the moment would take some practice," said William.

"Yes, it does. To really appreciate being in the moment, you're not thinking about yesterdays and tomorrows. You're not living in the past and imagining the uncertainties of the future."

"But isn't knowledge of what happened in the past necessary to plan for the future?"

"Understanding the experience of the past and the possibilities of the future while being fully present is where you'll find your passion and your purpose. So you see, William, planning isn't the problem. The problem is that we're usually thinking of things not related to what we're doing in the moment. Our attention is elsewhere. Some of the barriers to being fully present in the moment and that cause much of our suffering are longing, doing too much for too long, over indulging, being over stimulated and generally living excessively. We tend to *do* too much and not *live* enough."

"That's me," William laughed. "Have you been spying on me?"

"It's not just you," Charmaine said, winking. "We all do it."

"Well, that's comforting - I think."

"Usually," she continued, "the pilot running the show is our 'reactive' or 'conditioned' mind, or the 'ego'. When the conditioned mind is in gear, we tend to behave either from past memory or future uncertainty. This seems necessary to our ego in order to stay in control and feel safe. But the ego tends to judge, compare, label and assign fault or blame. It promotes fear in our lives. A mind *not* fully in the moment makes us susceptible to worry, anxiety, regret, depression, guilt and resentment. That robs us of the chance to appreciate what's happening in the present, which if you will remember, is all there is."

"Living in the moment would certainly simplify things, wouldn't it?" William asked as he imagined living his own life a moment at a time.

"It has for me," said Charmaine. "But our ego colors it in ways that rob the magic from the moment. The more thinking we do, with our conditioned mind running the show, the further from the moment we get, from the natural flow of our life. Our mind wants to escape from the moment so it can feel in control. And to the degree our ego is at the controls is the degree we are likely to miss the full impact and meaning of the present, which again..."

"...is all we have," William finished her sentence like a student who has done his homework.

"So, if we aren't aware of what's going on in our mind, we end up floating through life on auto pilot."

"But don't we sometimes need to be on auto-pilot," William asked. "That's what allows me to do more than one thing at a time, like driving to work while thinking about something far away."

"Yes." Charmaine replied. "There's nothing wrong with being on auto pilot. It can actually be a very efficient way to operate. The idea here is to be aware of being on auto-pilot. We can learn to be aware of our thoughts, especially the ones that keep playing over and over in our heads. What happens *inside you* is much more important than what happens *outside you*."

"Hmm," he said reflectively. "That's worth thinking about."

"So it's important to be conscious of your thoughts. Notice when you're thinking about the past or the future so you can interrupt unproductive rambling and redirect it to the present. Develop the habit of moving away from continual and incessant negative patterns of thinking so that you are alert and totally *with* what's happening now. Being present to your own experience of life as it is happening can produce wonderful results."

"Like what?"

"Remember, we find our peace and clarity in moments of now. It's in the present moment that we are in touch with our intuition, our creativity, our gentleness and our strength. This place is the very source of our life energy and our real power. It is in the moments of now where you will find the *doorway* to your soul!"

"Is there an easy way to get into the moment?" William asked. "I understand the inner mind stuff a little bit more now, but do you know a practical way to get there?"

"Well, besides being a witness to your thoughts, you could be a witness to your body," Charmaine suggested.

William turned and looked wryly at the extra weight he knew he was carrying. "I witness my body all right. Every day in the mirror!"

Charmaine chuckled. "That's not exactly what I had in mind. Body awareness - free of judgment of how you feel or how you look - can also keep you in touch with yourself in moments of now. It's a foolproof way to get out of those fruitless think-cycles we sometimes get caught up in."

"How'd you know I do that?"

"We all do it," she said, patting him gently on the shoulder. "Just take a moment to feel the energy within yourself."

"Now?"

"Sure. One excellent way to tune into your body is to focus your attention on your breathing."

William closed his eyes and took a deep, relaxing breath. "Okay, I'm focusing."

"Notice what parts of your body move as you allow your body to ef-fortlessly breathe itself. If you can identify with the *observer - the witness deep within*, rather than with *what you are observing* - your physical body, for just even a few moments, you may notice you don't actually have to think about breathing at all. Your body knows how to breathe just fine, without any help from you. You become the loving witness from way deep down inside, simply noticing what it feels like to allow your body to breathe itself. Especially focus your attention on the naturalness of your exhalations. Practice softening and letting go with each breath."

"What has to soften? I'm not sure how to do that."

"Soften your eyes, your tongue and your belly. To soften your eyes, close them and then imagine gazing effortlessly, allowing them to be out of focus with nothing to see. To soften your tongue, imagine allowing it to become heavy and loose in your mouth. It's just lying there with nothing to say. There's a feeling of releasing any tension and simply letting go. Just see if you can willingly let go of any tension especially in those areas of your body. If you feel *willing* to soften but your body doesn't seem to be cooperating, it's sometimes helpful to first really tighten all the muscles around your eyes, tongue and belly. Then take a breath and soften again as you let go of holding on to your breath. Softening those areas can be a key to relaxing your entire body. And you really can't mentally and emotionally 'let go' and get fully present if your body is 'up tight'.

"And how do I 'let go' of a breath?"

"Letting go of a breath is neither to hold back the exhalation nor to force it out. Simply allow your breath to naturally *fall* out of your body."

"I think I can do that, Charmaine. That's like doing nothing. Just let it happen on its own."

"Exactly. Focus your attention on your body when you're at work, in your relationships and even when you're enjoying beauty, like a magnificent sunset. For example, I notice that when I think I'm listening to another person, if I'm not exhaling effortlessly, I'm really not listening. I'm either waiting, judging or comparing. Use your breath as an indicator of your availability to be truly present to yourself or to others. Notice what happens when you feel anxious, worried, depressed or angry, and what your conditioned mind is thinking that causes those feelings."

"Oh," William said. "You don't want to know what I think when I feel that way!"

"What happens in your body when you feel anxious, for example?"

"Let's see, well, for starters I can see that I'm probably holding my breath. I sometimes start pacing, I often lose my appetite and my heart races, I guess."

"Isn't it usually when you're resisting, judging, being impatient or making unfair comparisons that you feel this way?"

"Yes, I suppose... What are you getting at, Charmaine?"

"Body awareness. Your body will tell you a lot about what's going on. For example, when you are anxious, worried, afraid or angry, notice the dryness in your mouth, or the tightness in your eyes, your jaw or your belly. Notice if there is a heaviness in your chest or a tiredness in your shoulders. Notice if there is a pounding in your head. Practice paying attention to signals from your body. Learn to recognize when your body is tight and when it is relaxed. Awareness is the key to choosing to *let go* and being more fully present."

"But how do I do it?"

"It's not a *doing*. Actually, it's more of an *un-doing* - a letting go of doing anything. There really is nothing to *do*. It's about *being* the witness. Take a breath and as you exhale begin to lovingly notice your body telling you what it is feeling. Be a witness to your physical sensations. As a loving witness you do not add any judgments or comparisons. There is no resistance to whatever you are aware of. You can have your physical and emotional symptoms or they will have you. Again, awareness is the key. It is in that awareness that you will find your clarity and your joy. You'll know you are being more fully present in a moment of now by the sense of peace you feel within."

"So," William said, a little troubled, "are you saying I'd be a better person if I were present in every moment of now? That seems impossible!"

"No. First of all, there's nothing wrong with who you are - or who any of us are. Remember, we're spiritual beings living in physical bodies. Our deepest nature has a Divine source. It is in our frailty as earthly creatures that we find all our flaws and struggles. But there is nothing wrong with who we are at the Divine core of our being. Not a thing."

"Thank you, Charmaine. I needed to hear that!"

"Secondly, as creatures on this earth, it would be extremely uncommon to be fully present *all* the time. That would be what's called 'having your act together' or 'total enlightenment'. I don't know of too many people who have 'arrived'."

"You seem pretty enlightened to me!" said William.

"Oh, I've been working on this for a long time and can assure you I don't even remotely have my act together. I just know that the more fully aware and present I am in moments of now, the better my life works."

"That's the whole point, isn't it?"

"Absolutely. And once you grasp its simplicity, you'll be surprised to find you can experience more moments of now than you would have ever imagined!"

"But I think," Charmaine continued, "it's important not to make ourselves wrong for not being fully present all the time. It's a part of our human condition in the real world. There are many factors that can affect your ability to be fully present."

"Such as...?"

"Well, for me it's important to get enough rest and to be physically active. And it makes a lot of difference if I spend some time each day in prayer or meditation or any centering practice that is designed to help me be more fully present. Volunteering and helping others in the community keeps me connected to something bigger than myself. And I like to write every day about what's going on in my heart and my busy little mind."

"How is writing every day helpful?"

"It frees up space in my head, creating room for me to think about other things. It helps to remind me to be grateful for what I have. It encourages me to be more clear about what I'm thinking and feeling. Our ego sometimes has a little disorder I call 'fuzziphelia'. It's the 'fear of getting clear'. For example, our ego is afraid that if it got clear about what it really wants our ego would find out it can't have it. Or if our ego got clear about what it felt about a relationship, it might have to face doing something it's afraid to do."

"Clarity has its own power, William. The more present I am, the more clear I am and the more effective I am in all things. This is true even if the anticipation of facing things appears difficult or scary to my ego."

"Does that seem like a lot to think about?" Charmaine asked. "Let's walk so we can practice being silently present in the moment. You've heard phrases like 'Stop and smell the roses' or 'Feel the pavement beneath your feet'. Those notions are at the heart of being fully in the moment. Take in everything your eyes can see. Hear the subtle and not so subtle sounds. Notice your breathing. Be aware of all your physical sensations as you walk. Feel the energy around you. If you can be fully present in the moment you'll experience the tranquility and peace. You'll just feel better, William!"

They came to the tree-lined street near his place.

"Would you like to see the flowers in my yard? They need some weeding but they're pretty." They walked along the sidewalk to William's place. William paused and looked at his home and neighborhood as if for the first time. Late afternoon sunlight lightly brushed a cluster of golden lilies on the far side of the house next to his. He'd never really noticed them before. A feeling of warmth and safety flooded his heart as he gazed at his home and the neighborhood surrounding him.

"I've taken too much for granted about this place I call home. I haven't really been present to my neighbors. It's like I'm seeing it with brand new eyes."

"When you are fully present in the moment, you bring a different kind of value and meaning to what you do. If you pay total attention to simply *what is,* without interpretation or judgment, it gives you the power and the clarity to do your best and find your strengths. You'll find it easier to be motivated, inspired and confident. You will be humble enough to share with others. You will see if, when and how to take appropriate action. You'll know when to let go of the things that don't really matter. You'll know when and how to stand tall on the things that do matter. Do you think it might make a difference in how you feel about your work, too?"

"It sure might be interesting to find out."

William picked a scarlet zinnia from the flowers his landlady had planted beside the front walk and handed it to Charmaine. A gentle wind swirled around them. Charmaine's flowing skirt shifted in the breeze. She tucked the flower behind her ear and pirouetted to her own rhythms. William was charmed by her natural beauty and expression of total freedom.

"So, William, what were you aware of during our walk?"

"It was weird to notice everything I was thinking and feeling. You know, the more present I am in moments of now, the more time just seems to open up - like it's bigger. It feels like each moment contains more. Does that make sense, Charmaine?"

"It does indeed. In fact, *in this world of physical reality the more totally present you are in any given moment of now is as close to forever as you will ever get.* Forever is not *out there* somewhere, years down the road. Forever can only be experienced in a moment of now."

"Oh, I like that! *Forever* tucked deeply into each moment of now..."

"Nicely put, William. To be more fully present in any given moment of now requires two things."

"What's that?"

"First, it requires a *skillful act of will*. It is a conscious choice of letting go of the illusion of being in control and accepting that living in the moment is life-changing in a very positive way."

"Second, it requires a *willingness to surrender* - to temporarily suspend *holding on* to things mattering, letting go of the *illusion* of control. Surrender your criticalness of the circumstances that you can't do anything about. Surrender your judgments of people who have a right to be who they are."

"Surrender is not about letting go *forever*. Surrender is about *totally* letting go in a moment of now. Our ego thinks surrender is forever - that it's death itself, so it will try its best to get us not to do it. Our ego thinks surrendering will cause us to lose something, to risk giving up a part or all of who we are. It is afraid it will become weak and vulnerable. But it's just the opposite. Our ego thinks it is us and thinks its survival depends on staying in control, which is an illusion. It also thinks its survival depends on getting what it needs and wants out in the world of physical reality."

"Charmaine, can you explain more about what you mean by *ego* and *soul*. I'm feeling there is something important in this for me but I'm a little confused. I think I'm beginning to understand the *gift of suffering* even though I can tell it will take practice to surrender to the full extent of my feelings. And I can see that a moment of now is like one frame in the movie that is my life. I also am beginning to see the positive things that can come out of being more present. But this ego - soul thing is pretty much going right past me."

"Would you like an apple?" she asked as she reached deep into her backpack. "It's off my own dwarf Gravenstein."

"Thanks! Mmm, it smells like a real apple!"

"You know what," Charmaine said, "I think you have enough to ponder and practice for one day. Want to meet here tomorrow, late afternoon? You can show me the bridge that overlooks the city below and I'll explain 'soul' and 'ego' in a way that I think you will understand. One reason that some of this seems so confusing is because many of the Eight Clues overlap. It's difficult talking about one of them without referring to the others. I think you'll see that it will begin to make more sense as we go."

"Sounds good to me. I'll see you tomorrow."

Summary

Clue #2 : "Live Your Life in Each Moment of Now."

Being present and living in the moment is being totally absorbed and involved with all of your senses in the present. It's not living in the past nor is it imagining the uncertainties of the future. Living in moments of now frees you from judging, comparing, labeling and assigning credit or blame. Being totally present and living in the moment relieves fear, worry, anxiety and life stress.

- Each frame of 'your' movie is a moment of now. It is actually a flow with no lines between the frames.

- Be wholly absorbed and involved with all of your senses in the present.

- Be free of living in the past or imagining the uncertainties of the future.

- Living in the moment frees us from judging, comparing, labeling and assigning fault or blame, without losing our capacity for discernment.

- You can learn to be aware of your thoughts and your body's feelings.

- Use your breath to help you to let go and feel the moment.

- Being fully present in a moment of now is as close to forever as you will ever get.

- Living in the moment requires a skillful act of will to let go of the illusion of being in control.

- Living in the moment requires a willingness to surrender your judgments for the moment.

- Not being present in moments of now causes worry, anxiety, regret, depression, guilt and resentment.

- Get enough rest. Exercise regularly. Spend some time each day in prayer or meditation. Write each day about what is going on in your heart and your mind. Find some way to express yourself daily through art, dance, music or nature.

At Work

- Living in the moment is when you are totally conscious on the job and doing your best.

The Benefits of Understanding Living in Moments of Now

You will find peace and clarity in moments of now. You will get in touch with your intuition, your creativity, your gentleness and your strength. Simply, your life will work better. Once you have this concept you will be surprised to find you can experience being fully present in more moments of now than you would ever have imagined.

Exercise

1: "A Meditation"

This exercise is designed to help you let go and be more fully present in moments of now. At first give yourself at least 10 or 15 minutes to do this exercise. The more frequently you do this meditation the more you will be able to get into a peaceful state of being in a few minutes or even a few seconds.

The more you get into doing this meditation the more you will begin to see positive results in your life. You will notice that you naturally begin to take things a little less seriously (without losing your passion for living); you will notice you begin to take things less personally; you will notice you are listening better and are more willing to speak up and ask for what you want; you may notice your intuition is more available to you; and you are more creative in your problem solving. As you get more comfortable with the process, you may want to spend more time with it.

Step 1: Get in a comfortable position. Let your body be as symmetrical as possible. (The more physically aligned your body is, the easier it is for your mind, body and spirit to be aligned as one.)

Step 2: Take a breath. Begin to focus all your awareness and attention on the coming in and falling away of each breath. Don't force it in or out. Simply allow your body to breath itself.

Step 3: Feel free to readjust your body in any way that feels comfortable while keeping it as symmetrical as possible.

Step 4: Begin to notice what parts of your body move as you allow your body to breathe itself effortlessly. Invite all your physical sensations to be there, exactly as they are, neither pushing them away nor holding onto them.

Step 5: Be the loving observer, the witness deep within. Think of yourself as the peaceful one watching your own body breathing itself.

Step 6: Practice softening with each breath. Soften your eyes, your tongue and your belly. To soften your eyes, close them and gaze effortlessly, with nothing to see. To soften your tongue, allow it to become heavy and loose in your mouth, with nothing to say. To soften your belly, bring your awareness to your abdomen and surrender, just even for a moment, to all of life - exactly the way it is. Lovingly think "soft belly", "soft, soft belly".

Step 7: If you feel *willing* to soften but your body does not seem to be co-operating, it is sometimes helpful to first tighten all the muscles around your eyes, your tongue, your belly or any other place where there seems to be some tightness or resistance. Feel free to rub, squeeze or stretch those areas of your body. The distraction will usually pass away, but if they don't, then simply invite them to be there exactly as they are. Now take a breath and soften again as you allow the air to simply fall out of your body, neither pushing it away nor holding on to it.

Step 8: Notice any sounds you may hear. Lovingly invite the sounds into your awareness exactly as they are with no resistance or objection to them being there. Allow the sounds to simply flow through your awareness just like your breath - neither pushing them away nor holding on to them.

Step 9: Notice any smells or odors that come into your awareness. Stay present and lovingly invite them to be there. Just like your breath, just like your physical sensations, just like the sounds, simply allow the scents to flow through your awareness, neither pushing them away nor holding on to them.

Step10: Now begin to lovingly notice any thoughts your mind might be having and any feelings or images that may arise. Invite them to be there exactly as they are - with no resistance or objection to them at all. If you notice a critical thought, then just lovingly notice that your mind had that thought. Allow your thoughts, like your breath, like your physical awareness, like the sounds, like the smells to simply flow through your awareness, neither pushing them away, nor holding on to them. There is nothing to *do* now. Just *be* the the loving witness from deep within - fully present in each moment of now.

Step 11: As a second phase of this exercise, take this practice out into your world. Go for a walk outside, preferably someplace quiet like a park or a garden. Again, begin by focusing on your breath. Stand comfortably still for a few moments. Lovingly notice whatever comes into your awareness from all of your senses. Begin to move slowly and notice the sensations of your body moving forward. Feel the souls of your feet stretching out and touching the ground under you. Notice the sound of your breath, the rustle of leaves, the sounds of other people and activities. Invite them all to be there exactly as they are, free of any judgments or comparisons. Allow all the sights, sounds, smells and the physical sensations to simply flow through your awareness, neither pushing them away, nor holding on to them.

Step 12: Imagine taking this state of being with you while you're driving. Keep focusing on your breath and on softening.

Step 13: Now imagine taking this state of being with you to work. Take it with you everywhere you go. Notice what begins to happen as you keep focusing on your breath and softening.

Principle

"Stop and smell the roses. Feel the ground beneath your feet." There is an old saying which invites you to be fully present in the moment. Having some daily exercise or centering practice will have a cumulative and positive effect on your life. It is a way to gradually deepen the baseline from which you experience your life, moment to moment. This meditation is designed specifically to help you become more fully present in each moment of now at home, at work and when you're alone.

#2: "Free Writing"

There are many forms personal journaling can take. This is a form that focuses on the free flow of you thoughts, a journaling of your stream of consciousness. Pick a quiet, comfortable well-lit space where you will not be disturbed by background sounds or activities. It helps to do this exercise in the same place and at the same time each day. Being in this familiar environment is not a requirement but you will notice that it will help to free the flow of your thoughts and ideas.

Some people are more creative in the morning, while many people have more energy in the evenings. It doesn't matter when you write... just do it. Many people notice that the content seems to flow more deeply if they write by hand rather than use a computer. See which works best and feels most natural to you. Give yourself 10-15 minutes a day to do this reflective exercise. Don't worry about your grammar or your composition. It doesn't matter how it looks.

Step 1: Sit quietly for a moment. Get comfortable. Begin by closing your eyes and taking a few easy breaths.

Step 2: Pick up your pen or pencil and start to write about anything that is in your awareness. Notice any distracting thoughts of feelings and write them down with no editing or censoring. Be as clear and specific as possible. This sometimes feels a little like peeling an onion, layer by layer: you won't know what is underneath until you write exactly what is on top.

Step 3: Continue to focus your attention on your breathing as you write. Become a loving witness to the thing observed, the flow of your thoughts, feelings and sensations, even as you write them down. Just let them all pour out! Don't worry if they make sense or not.

Step 4: If you choose to take a specific issue into your journaling, write down your feelings when particular events occurred and how you reacted to them. Be exact; be honest with yourself. Journaling is also a great opportunity to ask yourself questions about where you're going, what you really want out of life, why you struggle with certain problems and what things seem to make you unhappy, stressed, lonely or angry. Then see if you can find the answers for the questions.

Principle

Writing down your thoughts forces you to articulate them into specific words. It is a way to get access to your deeper clarity and to express the feelings associated with the ideas. Expressing thoughts and feelings is a way to process them and thereby move through them and get free from any difficulties they may have caused you. In time you will find that you will see a pattern in your thoughts, feelings and experiences, and you will begin to get new insights into why you react a certain way. Journaling, like physical exercise or meditating on a regular basis, is a soul nurturing activity and over time has a powerful and positive cumulative effect.

Chapter Five

Clue # 3

Learn to Choose Soul Over Ego, Love Over Fear.

As William and Charmaine walked toward the bridge late the next afternoon, he spotted a fast food place.

"Mmmm. That looks like my dinner calling out to me."

They stopped and William decided to get a small salad to go instead of his usual fried foods. Normally, he would really pack it away. But today he ate more peacefully, only eating what he needed to ease his hunger. He actually took the time to enjoy the texture and flavor of each mouthful.

"You know, I guess I've been on auto-pilot so much I've never really paid much attention to the food I eat. I just get it in my mouth and swallow it as fast as I can so I can shove some more in. These vegetables are actually pretty tasty. I guess that's the point, isn't it, to feel and be more aware of everything each moment?"

"There's a lot to be found in those moments of now when we are more fully aware, William." Charmaine nodded as she bent down to smell a fragrant flower. "Imagine how staying in the moment might affect all the difficult situations at your job. You might notice that you listen better. You would be more able to set boundaries - to say 'no' to things that don't feel right, and be able to let go of things that don't really matter. You might notice how others react no longer has the power to determine how you feel. You might become a more creative problem-solver. Your intuition will better guide you about when and how to bring things up to your boss. There's no end to the kind of positive changes you might see."

They continued their walk to the bridge, marveling at the constant movement of the city, filled with delicious scents of flowers and freshly cut grass. William noticed the vibrant colors and all the various sounds. He admired the effects of the late afternoon sunlight streaming through the skyline of buildings. Charmaine noticed her ankle was still sore from her tendency to see how fast she could take a corner . She did like to roller blade on the 'edge'.

As they reached the bridge, William turned to Charmaine.

"Tell me about the third Clue - about the soul and the ego."

They sat down together on a bench and gazed at the beginning of what would become a glorious sunset over the distant mountains beyond the city. They were quiet for a while.

"This is truly a special place,William. Thank you for bringing me here."

"It's nice to have a friend to share it with, Charmaine."

The Soul (Love)

"William, I invite you to consider how we are all 'wired up'. Imagine looking at it this way. You have a mind and you have a body. But you are not your mind and you are not your body. There is a bigger, deeper you that *has* your mind and body. This deeper you is what I call the soul. When I speak of the soul I am referring to that aspect of our being, in fact, the very essence of our being, which connects us to all of life, each other, the earth and all its creatures and to the Source. I refer to the soul by many words and phrases such as spirit, inner or higher self, deeper self, our big mind, the loving witness within, the open heart. I consider it to be our access point to the Divine, the Source. The soul is beyond the realm of the intellect and the mind/body. It is beyond finite definition. Our words can only point to it. It is not measurable in the science of physical reality. It is bigger than that. In fact, physical reality only exists in the context of the Divine."

"We all have access to a shared and very real experience of this Source. We may or may not be consciously aware of this *connectedness* but it is very real. It is, and we are part of, the Mystery. This deeper awareness is never caught up in the future or the past. It is totally present. There is no fear in this place because there is nothing to be afraid of. There is no loneliness because there is nothing from which the soul is separate. This is not a physical place in your body. It is the essence of every cell that has ever been in your body. You can experience this place when your heart is open to life and you are fully present. It is possible to learn how to cultivate a deeper and more frequent awareness of this Divine presence."

"At any given moment of now, it all depends on whether you identify with your ego, your mind/body or whether you identify with your soul, the loving witness deep within.

Each moment of now is a *totally new opportunity* to either open your heart and live from your soul or to close off and remain stuck in your ego with all its symptoms. Getting to inner peace is *not* about creating peacefulness. It is about learning how to choose to go to the place where your natural peacefulness is always waiting."

"And where is that?"

"Your soul, William. Being fully present in a moment of now feels like falling in love – with life."

The Ego (Fear)

"I think of the ego as our mind/body in physical reality. It's the part of us that thinks it is us. I think of the ego as our conditioned mind, our little mind, as differentiated from our big mind, our universal mind - our soul," Charmaine continued.

"Our ego is always based in fear, scarcity and separation. Our ego, in its innocent but misguided way, only knows to look out in the world of physical reality or at itself for all the problems and their solutions. It's wrong on both counts. Always, the problems - or suffering - come when we identify with our ego rather than our soul. All our suffering comes from the attachments our ego has formed out in the world."

"Do you mean that our ego always thinks the problems and solutions in life are either out in the world or with itself, like if it would just grow up or not be so clumsy or get this amount of money or that relationship, whatever... then everything would be okay?" William asked.

"That's right. But remember, our ego is not the enemy. It is completely innocent and yet totally misguided in its commitment to the notion that its survival depends on staying in control. Our ego thinks that control is necessary for it to find happiness out in the world, the only place it knows to look."

"Charmaine, so what good is the ego? It sounds like it's the source of all my problems."

"The value of the ego is that it is the mechanism by which the Source creates the unique and inescapable opportunities for each of us to do the healing work we came here to do. There is a purpose to life, William. Think of life as a healing journey. Each of us is infinitely unique, like each grain of sand, each leaf, each snowflake. The ego is the *predetermined* pallet from which we exercise our *free will* to paint the living picture that is our life. The usefulness of the ego is that it can't help but lead us to the joys and the sufferings of our life, depending on how we exercise our free will. We either learn through joy or we learn through suffering. That expression of free will forms our life's healing journey."

The Illusion of Control and Fear

"Actually, control is an illusion. We have never been in control for a moment in our entire lives. Control is a mechanism designed by our ego for its own survival. Our ego thinks its survival depends on it being and staying in control. One of the ways our ego does this is by holding on to its evidence and being right. It would generally rather be right than get what it said it wanted in the first place - to be happy."

"The mechanism our ego uses to try to stay in control is by our fear-based thoughts. Its favorite strategy for staying in control, therefore, is to avoid certain intense or unpleasant feelings. That's because from our ego's point of view, if we are feeling intense feelings we are not going to be in control. And isn't it interesting that it's these very thoughts that actually cause us to feel our fearful, insecure feelings?"

"You mean, if we were in an intensive care unit, brain dead, no cerebral activity, flat-lined, we would not be feeling any feelings?"

"Exactly. *For us to have a feeling we need to have a thought.* The feelings that come from fearful thoughts include anger, greed, resentment, guilt, vindictiveness, spite, jealousy, arrogance, boredom, impatience and criticalness of ourselves and others. They also include many kinds of anxieties, depressions, phobias and obsessions. The list goes on and on and on. And if you chase these fearful thoughts down, you will find they always take you to the same place: *a fear of loss of love.* It is fear of being alone, abandoned, not seen, not safe and not connected to anything or anyone."

"Another of our ego's favorite strategies for staying in control is to try to figure out why we are feeling a specific feeling. It thinks that if it could figure out why we are feeling something it would not actually have to feel it, thereby losing control."

"And here is an interesting little irony, William. The ego's desire to stay in control comes out of its desire to finally feel safe, secure and free. The irony is that when it finally is willing to surrender the *illusion* of control and allow the soul's Divine love into its awareness, we feel a *natural* sense of being safe, secure and free."

"So," said William, "when I *let go*, I feel the very love my ego was looking for in the first place. Geez, my ego must be very afraid. It really is *totally* misguided."

"William, it sounds like you're experiencing compassion for your ego right now, aren't you?"

"I guess I am."

"While we're on the subject of *control*, here's a concept you might want to think about William: *all fear is illusion*."

"Fear is an illusion, too?" he asked, amazed. "Fear feels pretty real to me!"

Charmaine smiled. "Have you ever had a bad dream – a real nightmare?"

"Well, sure. Lots of them, especially lately. Why?"

"What makes it a bad dream is that first, you don't know you are dreaming. It seems very real. Second, you can never seem to get away from the boogieman or the boogie situation. But what works when you're having a bad dream?"

"Waking up," he answered.

"And when you wake up what do you say to yourself?"

"Thank God it was just a bad dream!"

"You are really saying it had no reality at all. It was all inside your head – just thoughts originating in your mind. When you are struggling in your life, William, you are effectively just having a bad dream. You simply think you are awake."

"No kidding!"

"It's all in your head. They are just thoughts coming from your fearful, insecure mind. This is true even though those fearful thoughts can seem very real."

"Hmmm, I need to think about that," he said. "If fear is an illusion... what's all the fuss? Why do we put so much energy into worrying about stuff that's not real?"

Charmaine laughed. "The *stuff* is real – but your reaction to it, the meaning you bring to it, creates peace or pain. Your choice. So, the less fear you call up, the more energy you will have for living well and the more free you will feel."

"Here's another interesting thing, speaking of freedom. An interesting definition of freedom is *being in a moment of now in which there is no feeling you are afraid to experience.*"

"That's another good one. Where do you get all these little ditties?"

"The reason that some of these ditties, as you call them, resonate with you is that it's only on the surface that we're all different. At the core of our being we all share the same spiritual knowing. But to answer your question, I think these little ditties simply come from spontaneous thoughts over many years of practicing the Clues."

Power

"There are two kinds of power, William. There is soulful power and there is egoic power. The ego's power is always based in scarcity. It only exists in the finite and closed system of the ego. For you to have more, someone else always has to have less. Soulful power is based in an infinite and open system of abundance. It doesn't require anyone else to have less for you to have more. In fact, the more everyone has the better.

The Dance

"Gee, it sounds like our ego is afraid of not ever finding what we already have inside us." William said.

"That's really the heart of the matter,"Charmaine agreed. "And the implications of that moment-to-moment dance between the soul and ego is what makes up the quality of our experience of everything and everyone in our life. Finding your soul occurs when the ego allows the soul's love into the moment. It happens as our ego begins to see that *surrendering* is a safe thing to do. The kind of *surrendering* we are talking about here is not surrendering to anything or anyone out in the physical world. It is the ego momentarily releasing its grip on the illusion of control. It is the ego surrendering to the soul."

"So, there is a soulful, spirit-based place inside each of us where we're always at peace, safe, secure, clear, strong, gentle and wise. I like the sound of that."

"If we are not experiencing those things in our life, William, it's not because they're not there. It's because we're not where they are. It's an inward journey and there are tools of both *understanding* the mechanisms and tools of *practice* that can help us spend more of our life coming from that place. It's the dance between the soul and the ego. *And it happens in every moment of now in our entire lives, whether we are aware of it or not.* It's what determines the quality of our life, moment-to-moment. We naturally already experience more time in this loving space than you might guess. It's just that when our hearts close and our ego's fear-based thoughts take over, life is so unpleasant that we just think it's most of the time."

"It sounds like our ego's intention is to find the love it's looking for in every place except where it really is." William said.

"Yes. It's an inward journey to the soul rather than an outward one somewhere in the world. Scarcity and loneliness are illusions. They are only thoughts from the ego's fearful and insecure perspective. In the soul there is no experience of loneliness because there is nothing from which you are separate. An open heart is the safest place in the world, William. All we will see is each other's innocence. By innocence I mean the soul's natural and absolute love, acceptance and compassion for everything including our ego. The soul sees the innocence of our ego's intentions."

"I've always thought of what you call the soul as my inner self," said William shyly, "but I have a hard time describing it or figuring out what it really means."

"Don't be confused or distracted by all the words I use to describe this essence. By its very nature, all the words in all the languages are inadequate to fully describe it. The words just point to it."

"You know, Charmaine, I think if I could just understand the nature of my soul and how to relate to it, my life would be smoother."

"Here's some good news for you, then," she said. "Can you now see that your soul is also your *personal access point* to the source of all life – the Infinite, the Divine, to what many people refer to as God?"

"My soul is my access point to God," he repeated thoughtfully.

"Think of it this way. We are spiritual beings who take birth into physical reality. We thereby enter into the illusion of separateness from the Divine, the source of infinite love. We naturally identify with our new physical world and our ego - our mind/body. The illusion of separateness is what happens every time we identify with our ego and physical reality rather than with our spiritual essence, our soul."

"When we innocently identify with our ego we inevitably experience a deep need to feel loved, safe, special and whole. We need an absolute guarantee of totally unconditional love in every moment of now for our whole lives. And from our ego's point of view we only see one direction to look for it - out in the world."

"But none of us ever get that kind of love for very long if at all, do we?"

"No, we don't, William. The problem is that we have taken birth into a world of physical reality that does not make the love we need in the size package we need it. That is, of course, except for every once in a while just long enough to suck our ego into thinking it really could find it out in the world. But then that source of love goes away, has to go to work, or is in a bad mood, or gets a better offer - or even dies. Now this may sound like a nasty little cosmic trick. We suffer at our inability to find the love we truly need and want. That suffering is trying to tell us something. It is telling us stop struggling out in the world. When we have finally suffered enough and finally do let go, we discover that through our soul we have access to the infinite and unconditional love that our ego was misguidedly looking for out in the world."

"Now imagine that at every moment ..."

"...of now," William interjected cheerfully.

"...yes, every moment of now," Charmaine smiled encouragingly, "there are only two possible experiences you can have. There is love, or there is fear. Another way to put it: there is soul or there is ego, open-heartedness or closed-heartedness. There is the big mind or the little mind. Living in balance or in a reactive state. Being centered or off-centered.

"Sounds like there are a lot of ways to describe it," said William.

"Actually, these are really several ways to say one thing – soul or ego."

"Is it really that simple?"

"Yes. This is one of life's great paradoxes. At the level of the ego and physical reality, life is so infinitely complex that you could never figure it out. At the level of the soul it is as simple as this: at every moment of now we are either coming from our soul or our ego. It can alternate between varying degrees of one or the other, but at each moment of now, it will always be either soul or ego taking the lead. And that is what determines the quality of our lives, from moment to moment."

"Think of it this way: at every moment of now we are either *coming from* love or we are *coming from* fear in terms of how we see ourselves, how we relate to each other and how we experience the world around us. You see, the quality of your life is not determined by what happens in the world, not by what we have or don't have or even by how others do or do not behave. Remember, the quality of your life, William, is totally determined by whether you identify with your ego or with your soul in each moment of now."

"Even if I completely mess up in one moment, I don't have to be discouraged, do I? *Because I have the next moment to make a choice that works better for me!*"

"Right," Charmaine agreed. *"You're not obligated to stick with a choice that doesn't work for you.* One moment of now doesn't define you any more than one frame in a movie makes an entire story."

"Now I understand what being a work in progress means," said William. "If I live with awareness, I am creating and re-creating myself each moment, aren't I?"

"Yes. And all the things in life that work come from that state of love, soul, or open-heartedness. What works are compassion, patience, forgiveness, mercy, tenderness, clarity, intuition, creativity, playfulness and wisdom. And our soul is also where we find not only our gentleness but our strength. *Herein lies our real power.* It is not power over anybody or anything, but a power that comes from a groundedness, a centeredness, a clarity that has its own power."

"The things that come from fear are not bad or evil. It's just that when we get stuck in them, our life doesn't work very well. Fear breeds anger, greed, resentment, guilt, vindictiveness, shame, spite, jealousy, arrogance, boredom, anxieties, phobias, obsessions and depression."

"Sounds like a description of my life," muttered William.

"Most people's lives. Anger, for example, is a very common experience. Think of a moment when you were angry at your boss..."

"I can think of dozens of moments like that! My jaws get tight just thinking about them!"

"You know, the anger isn't the primary or even secondary emotion."

"It isn't?"

"No. Any time you're angry or see someone else who is angry, beneath that anger you will always find hurt. The anger can be so ugly, toxic or even lethal that it's sometimes hard to see the hurt under the anger. Yet, if you could clearly see the hurt, you would also see a kind of innocence about it."

"Like an injured lion cub who strikes at anything that comes near," William nodded.

"Look under the hurt and you will find fear."

"Always?"

"Always...and here's the kicker. If you look under the fear, you will find that it always takes us to the same place - fear of loss of love. We humans fear being rejected and abandoned. We fear not being seen or respected and appreciated because we need to be included and held as special. All the negative stuff that comes from our ego's fear-based angry thoughts are part of an innocent but misguided strategy for love or survival."

"So the angriest among us are really just very hurt and afraid."

"That's true. And here's the point. Until we realize that the love and security we all long for only comes through an inward journey, we are bound to be stuck in our suffering."

"Where do I buy a ticket, then? I need to take this journey!"

"You already have a ticket. Once you learn to tap into your inner access to love, you will discover an amazing thing. Now pay attention my friend. If you remember nothing else we've talked about, *remember this:* you bring that love and security *to* your life, *to* all of your activities and relationships instead of trying desperately to find it *in* them."

"That is amazing! If that's true, I really do get to write my own ticket to happiness without looking for it in some *one* or some *thing* else! So tell me more about how to write my own ticket."

"Ok, let's get practical," Charmaine said. "It's important to understand how we are *wired up*. It's possible to develop your awareness so you can begin to notice when your heart is open and when it is not."

"Like a sign that says 'Open' or 'Closed'?"

"Just like that. Although it's relatively easy to see in others, it's a little trickier to see in ourselves. To have awareness, it's necessary to take a step back. That's why practices that help develop our ability and inclination to lovingly observe our own thoughts, feelings and physical sensations are so important."

"Practices like meditation?"

"That's what is most helpful to me. It helps me learn to open my heart."

"So opening my heart is a *learnable* skill?"

"Absolutely. Here is where the rubber meets the road. Once you begin to notice when your heart is open and when it's not, you can begin to choose, in some moments of now, to come from love rather than fear. I'm not suggesting that you can always do this in every single moment of now, but I assure you it is possible in more moments than you would ever imagine."

"Just increasing the percentage of time I live in moments of now would be worth it," William said hopefully.

"That is *my* goal," Charmaine said. "But it's important to understand that I'm not implying you would be a better person if you do this. It's just that everything in your life works better when you live from your soul rather than your ego. Remember, your ego is not the enemy. This is about opening your heart even to your own closed-heartedness."

"You mean, to be kind to that part of myself that believes in fear, control and scarcity?"

"Yes. Your ego isn't bad - it's part of who you are. This is where the experience of loving yourself, holding your ego with tenderness and mercy, can truly nourish and re-energize your life."

"If my heart is open - which sounds like another way to say vulnerable - and I'm coming from my soul, won't others see me as weak and try to take advantage of my gentleness?" asked William anxiously. "That could be a real problem where I work. It's so competitive there. Upper management even seems to pit us against each other!"

"That's a fair question." said Charmaine. "And the answer is no. That is just what it looks like to your ego as it *anticipates* letting go of its struggle. Nobody can *cause* you to feel pitted against anybody if you are coming from your center. Feeling pitted against someone can only come from your own ego's fearful, insecure thoughts."

"When you live and work from soulfulness, William, you are most effective in all the things you do. In this centered place you have access to your backbone as well as your gentleness. This is where you can temporarily set aside your own point of view to really hear others, because an open heart is free of your ego's attachments out in the world. You have access to your clarity and your wisdom. This is true in any crisis. It is true in any confrontation or dispute."

"From this open-hearted stance, you'll know when to let go of things that don't really matter and when to stand tall on the things that do. An open heart is not at all weak, but neither is it mean-spirited. Your soul is also where you will find your sense of timing and balance, your discernment and compassion, your intuition and your creativity. And how do you suppose you can get to this open-hearted place?"

"Let me guess. I already have the ticket to get there," William said, grinning.

"Good guess. You're getting it. All you have to do is take a breath and connect with that loving witness within."

The two friends sat quietly for a few more minutes as the sherbet orange of the sky turned to soft twilight blue. A single star pierced the transparent dome, as the moon rose to light their silhouettes on the bridge.

Summary

Clue # 3: "Learn to Choose Soul Over Ego, Love Over Fear."

We can learn to choose our soul rather than ego, love over fear, an open heart over a closed one, our 'big mind' over our 'little mind'. Which one you live your life from in each moment is ultimately what determines the quality of your life. The soul is your access point to the Source and all its gifts. The value of the ego is that it is the predetermined mechanism by which the Source creates the unique and inescapable opportunities for each of us to exercise our free will to do the growing and expanding work we came here to do. Understanding and consciously participating in the dance between the soul and ego and learning to choose between them is the key to soulful living.

Soul (Love)

- Our soul is who we really are, the very essence of our being.

- Our soul connects us to all of life and the Source.

- Our soul is the deeper, bigger *us* that contains within it our mind and our body – our ego.

- You can experience your soul when your heart is open to life and you are fully present.

- It is in our soul that we will find access to our clarity, intuition, timing, balance, wisdom, patience, discernment, creativity, gentleness and our backbone, our soulful power.

Ego (Fear)

- Our ego is our mind/body in physical reality.

- The value of the ego is that it is the mechanism by which the Source creates the unique and inescapable opportunities for each of us to do the growing and expanding work we came here to do.

- Our ego thinks it is us.

- Our ego is our conditioned mind, our little mind, our reactive mind.

- Our ego is always based in fear, scarcity and separation.

- Our ego is completely innocent but totally misguided.

- Our ego believes in the notion that its survival depends on staying in control.

- Our suffering comes when we identify with our ego rather than with our soul.

- All our suffering comes from the attachments our ego has formed out in the world.

- Our ego's fear-based thoughts are the source of all our fear-based feelings such as hurt, anger, guilt, resentment, vindictiveness, spite, jealousy and boredom.

- Our ego's fearful thoughts are basically the fear of loss of love.

- Practice opening your heart to your own closed-heartedness.

The Illusion of Control and Fear

- Control is an illusion. We have never been in control for a moment in our entire lives.

- Control is a mechanism designed by our ego for its own survival. Our ego thinks it is us and that its survival depends on being and staying in control. And it does this by way of fear-based thoughts. It is these thoughts that actually cause us to have fearful, insecure feelings.

- One of our ego's favorite strategies for staying in control is to avoid certain intense or unpleasant feelings. That is because from our ego's point of view, if we are feeling intense feelings we are not going to be in control.

- Another of our ego's favorite strategies for staying in control is to try and figure out why we are feeling a specific feeling. It thinks that if it could actually figure out *why* we are feeling something it would not actually have to feel it, thereby losing control.

- All fear is an illusion, just thoughts from our fearful, insecure 'little mind', like a bad dream.

- If you chase these fearful thoughts down you will find they always take you to the same place. It is a fear of loss of love. It is fear of being alone, abandoned, not seen, not safe and not connected to anything or anyone.

Power

There are two kinds of power in the world:

- There is *soulful power* which is based in an infinite and open system of Divine love. It does not require anyone else to have less for you to have more. In fact, the more everyone has, the better.

- There is *ego power* which is based in a finite and closed system of scarcity and separation. For anyone to have more somebody else has to have less.

The Dance

- We are spiritual beings who have taken birth into physical reality.

- We thereby enter into the illusion of separation from the Divine. This happens in every moment in which we identify with our ego rather than our soul.

- We all have a need for an absolute guarantee of totally unconditional love. When we innocently identify with our ego and physical reality we can only see one place to look for that love - out in the world.

- We have taken birth into a world that does not offer the love we need in the size package we need it.

- When we have suffered enough in our inability to find the love we need out in the world, we can learn to surrender the illusion of control and begin the inward journey to our access point to the infinite love from which we came.

- The quality of our lives is determined by whether we identify with our soul or our ego in each moment of now.

- Finding the love, safety and freedom for which we long is an inward journey to the soul rather than an outward journey somewhere in the world.

- Our ability and inclination to *lovingly* observe our own thoughts, feelings and physical sensations is a passage way to the soul.

- 'Awareness' is the most powerful agent of change.

At Work

- When you live from your soul at work you are most effective in all the things you do.

Understanding the Benefits of Learning to Choose Soul over Ego

Our ego breeds anger, greed, resentment, guilt, vindictiveness, shame, spite, jealousy, arrogance, boredom, anxieties, phobias, obsessions and depression.

Our soul is where we find our compassion, forgiveness, mercy, tenderness, clarity, intuition, creativity, playfulness, wisdom, gentleness and power.

Exercises

#1: "Practicing Defenselessness and Telling on Yourself"

This exercise is an example of one way to choose soul over ego. Imagine you are meeting your partner at the library at 7 pm. You arrive at 7:15. She is really angry and accuses you of being 20 minutes late (not 15). She says you've never been on time in your whole life and that nobody in your entire family has ever been on time. Practicing defenselessness is looking for the kernel of truth and acknowledging it. "The truth is I said I would be here at 7:00 and I wasn't." You totally ignore the parts that are overstated or completely untrue. (Your ego will struggle with letting go of correcting these untruths or pointing out one time when she was late.) You now tell on yourself. "Remember last week when we met for dinner at that Mexican restaurant, and I was about 10 or 15 minutes late for that as well?" You even offer information she would have no way of knowing. "In fact, I had lunch with a colleague today and I was about 10 minutes late for that as well."

Step 1: Get in a comfortable position. Sit quietly and take a few breaths.

Step 2: Identify some recent criticism that has been aimed at you about which you felt a little (or a lot) defensive.

Step 3: Now visualize the moment that it occurred. Recall the person, the time of day, the place and the circumstances. Recall the feelings that came over you at that moment. Invite those feelings fully into your awareness.

Step 4: Now take a breath and soften your body. See if you can identify a 'kernel of truth' in what was said. Let go of any part of the criticism that was untrue, unfair or inaccurate. Look only at the 'kernel of truth'.

Step 5: Now imagine facing that person and willingly, humbly acknowledging the truth of the criticism. Again, ignore any part of it that was untrue.

Step 6: (Not for the faint of heart) Now practice *telling on yourself.* Imagine telling that person another example of the thing about which they had criticized you. Tell them something they would have no other way of knowing and acknowledge that you can see why they were critical. (The anticipation of this will make your ego think it is going to die. It won't. It will be just fine.)

Principle

It is only our ego that ever needs defending or protecting. The soul is infinitely safe. Practicing *defenselessness* and *telling on yourself* can be a powerful way to step aside from your ego and align with your soul. The quality of your life depends upon your understanding the ongoing dance between the soul and the ego and learning to choose the soul in as many moments of now as you can.

2: "Media Celibacy"

We believe this exercise can help you create a living environment in which you can more easily identify with your soul. Our intention is to help you get off autopilot and become more conscious, aware and present to the moment. And that is where you can more easily connect with your soul. This exercise will also help you develop a more soul-nurturing relationship with whatever media you choose to have in your life. Our intention is to first make you more aware of the impact of the incessant and upsetting messages on certain radio and television shows and news programs, as well as all the marketing propaganda that you read, hear and see everyday. The influence of the media is one of the most powerful forces we encounter. It guides us in every way possible. Many of us feel we need to know what's going on, but more often than not, we find we're no longer thinking for ourselves. The media trains us to look outside ourselves, at products, entertainment or people of influence for the answers. Secondly, we want to invite you to make conscious choices about what, if any, media influences you choose to have in your life.

Step 1: In the first week of this exercise continue your life as normal but also begin to keep a daily log of the amount of time you spend listening, watching and reading the different media. It includes the number of hours you watch television, the times and hours you listen to the radio, how much time you're involved on the internet and the amount of time you spend looking at and reading newspapers, magazines or catalogues.

Step 2: In week two, cut the amount of time you spend with each medium by half. On your way to work listen to the radio if you like, but eliminate it on the way back home; let there be silence. Watch your favorite shows on television but cut back on other shows that aren't as much fun or as important to you. For many of us the internet is our main source of communication, so try cutting back to half the time.

Step 3: The third week watch a minimum of television (10 hours maximum) and definitely eliminate the local evening news. If you need to know the weather or the sports results, make sure that's the only part of the newscast you watch. Totally shut off the radio all week. Read only your Sunday newspaper. Only use the internet this week for friendly communication with your family and friends. Eliminate looking at the news or e-mails that try to sell you something. Do not read any magazines or catalogues this week.

Step 4: This week is only for the brave of heart! This is your first week of media celibacy. You will be watching no television, listening to no radio, reading nothing in the news and having no internet communications, even with your friends. Pay attention to signs of withdrawal and discomfort. You may notice other changes in your attitude and behavior.

Step 5: Repeat your new habit of week 4 for one more week. Try to live without the media for the entire week. Pay attention to a shift in how you are looking at the world around you. What do you notice?

Step 6: After six weeks return to what you were originally doing with every medium and notice the difference in the quality of your life. Begin to make a conscious choice about what amount and what forms of media you can have in your life that nurture your soul. Get off autopilot and be discerning and conscious in you choices.

Principle

You'll find that you'll be hearing and seeing things differently. You'll quickly realize how you can listen more effectively while catching the nuances and propaganda that the media uses to influence you. You'll find that you will not be as easily influenced by the emotional and cultural appeals of the constant marketing. The messages you read or hear you will now be able to balance more rationally with your real needs and wants. You will begin to slow down and evaluate the stream of information more rationally and it will eventually help you to be more at peace with who you are and what you need. You will begin to enjoy the silence and feel how calming it is.

As a great master, Paramahansa Yogananda, once said in *Autobiography of a Yogi,* "Environment is more powerful than will." So even though our will power is so strong that at any given moment it can overcome almost any environmental influence, hour by hour, day by day, month by month and year by year our environment has far more influence in our lives than our will. It is of profound importance to choose the influences in our life. Therefore, if you want to be healthier spend time with healthier people. If you want to be more spiritually grounded, then spend time in places where there are more spiritually grounded people. If you want more drugs in your life, hang out with people who use more drugs. If you want to become a better snow boarder, hang out with people who are even better than you are. If you want to be more peaceful, then spend time where there is more peacefulness. It matters what substances you put in your body, what you tend to place in front of your eyes, what sounds you invite into your ears, what people you surround yourself with. It matters what you allow to enter your every day world.

The media is not a benign stimulus.

Chapter Six

Clue # 4

Practice Loving Yourself

The bridge with the magnificent view, where William first began to open himself to his feelings, had become one of William and Charmaine's favorite places to talk. He always sensed the presence of something bigger than life when he looked out over the city below.

"I feel," he said, "like I'm seeing a real difference as I learn to apply the Clues to my everyday life. Remember my telling you about George, the fellow who always smiles and says hello when I pass him on the way home from work?"

"Sure I do." Charmaine nodded with interest.

"Well, yesterday I stopped and talked to him again. He's interesting and has a great sense of humor – a genuinely nice guy. He introduced me to his family and friends. They all seemed so happy. George and his wife Irene just had a new baby named Jacob, after his grandfather."

"Oh?"

"Yeah, the little guy looks just like his dad, especially the ears but I think he has his mother's eyes – just the sweetest, most precious little thing I've ever seen! I felt good just being near that little guy."

"Babies have that effect on us, don't they," said Charmaine.

"They're having a party to welcome him to the world and they want me to come. They even plan to have a softball game at the park after the party! Man, I haven't played softball in years. I told George about you and he smiled and said you should come too."

"Why, thanks for thinking of me, William! I think I will. Nice to see you getting out and about..."

"I've been reaching out to some of the people at work, too. And," he said with a sparkle in his eye, "I met a really interesting woman named Emily. She's a friend of Irene's."

"You're becoming quite the social butterfly!"

"What an unlikely picture *that* paints! But you know, I sometimes get frustrated with myself for being unable to apply what I'm learning from the Clues all the time. If I could just be more present – or more aware – or more open to my suffering, I'd reap the benefits of this ancient wisdom more consistently. I keep catching myself coming from my ego, you know, thinking with my 'little mind'. Any suggestions?"

"My first suggestion," Charmaine said, "is be fair and gentle with yourself. You can't expect to apply the wisdom from the Clues all the time. You'll be amazed how, with practice, it eventually becomes second nature to you. And yes, I do have a few other suggestions. But right now let's just watch the sun go down. Don't those colors just take your breath away!"

The flaming reds, subtle pinks and dusty lavenders looked like an airbrushed painting on the edge of the western sky. It was a *moment*, a moment of now for both of them. Everything was still. A lone bird sang one last note... a light breeze brushed softly by on its way to evening in the city.

Charmaine had felt William's frustration and understood it well. At times she felt impatient with herself, too.

"I think it's time to talk about the fourth Clue," she said, turning to her young friend.

"What is it?"

"It's about loving yourself."

"Loving yourself! It's conceited to love yourself. The people I know like that are arrogant, self-centered jerks. I don't want to be like them!"

"That's one of the forms it can take when the ego feels the need for love. That kind of self-centeredness actually reflects fear and insecurity. The ego thinks it's quite special and separate from others. But loving yourself in the way I'm talking about is what happens when the ego allows in and accepts the soul's Divine love. Then loving yourself is a very different thing."

"Oh."

"The soul loves the ego unconditionally, William, even with all its warts and wrinkles, with all of its strengths and weaknesses. Our ego's love for itself, on the other hand, is quite conditional and judgmental."

"I can relate to that," William said emphatically. "Oh, man, just the thought of how I tend to beat myself up makes me feel uncomfortable."

"You have difficulty forgiving yourself?"

"It's not my strong suit," William said regretfully. "Actually, I give myself a pretty hard time when I foul up. I wish I could be more... even."

"You mean *perfect*," asked Charmaine, smiling gently.

"Well, yeah...like some people I know."

"They probably wish the same thing."

"I just get so down when things don't work out. It makes me wonder if I'm not good enough. I feel especially discouraged when I don't get much respect from my boss."

"That would feel discouraging," Charmaine said, nodding sympathetically.

"I have moments when I don't like myself very much. I suspect if others knew me better they wouldn't like me either."

William shook his head as if to clear it.

"I'm feeling lousy again, just thinking about it. You know what? I have an almost overpowering urge to eat a carton of ice cream right now. How do I short-circuit – 'soul-robbing activities' like that? "

"Remember," she answered, "all those fearful insecure thoughts are exactly what's making you feel lousy again."

"I know... they come from my ego... my 'little mind'. I guess if I could embrace the idea of having fondness for my ego rather than demonizing it, my life would be less painful. If I have a little more compassion for my ego, I'll have more patience for it and be able to chuckle at its struggles. It'd be like watching little Jacob stumble and fall when he tries to stand or walk as he gets a little older. In the same way, I'd begin to see my mistakes with more patience and tenderness. I might begin to see my mistakes as simply experiences of learning to be in the world instead of feeling like I have to be perfect all the time."

"Let's start with you trying to be perfect," said Charmaine. "Consider the possibility that you *are* perfect."

"Oh, right!"

"Consider it, William," Charmaine repeated firmly. "Perfect, as you are. Could your 'little mind' be denying the Divine power that lies within you by rejecting the idea that you are indeed perfect in that place where your soul resides?"

"Huh?"

"And anyway, define 'perfect'! Perfect is different things to different people - a moving target. But we are all *perfect* at the soul level where we connect to the Divine. To deny that Divine presence is to lack self-love. And without self-love, we're unable to love others or receive their love in return."

William signed an emphatic 'time-out' with his hands.

"Are we talking religion, here," he asked, "because I'm not sure if I believe in Divine with a capital D."

"We're talking *spirituality* here," she answered, "because we're all spiritual beings, no matter how you define it. Let me explain it another way, then. Many people cling to the need to be perfect - at least to constantly strive to be. *But our soul, the part of us that is already perfect, loves the part of us that is not yet perfect - our ego.*

"Remember, you love the ones you love because of who they are, not because they're perfect. Treat yourself the same way. Let your heart be open to listening and understanding yourself. Be open to everyone's absolute right to be different and unique."

"We all have the *right* to be different and unique?"

"Well, of course," Charmaine chuckled. "William, you have as much value as anybody that has ever been born. We all do! It'd be a little arrogant to think you were special and unique by being the only one worth less."

William marveled at the simplicity of Charmaine's suggestion.

"So, just do my best to have an open heart? That seems like an easy way to start loving myself. But, some people seem able to do the right thing naturally," he added wistfully.

"I know it may often look like that, William. But comparing yourself to others is rarely in the service of loving yourself. When you do compare yourself with others you'll always find those that are better or worse than you are. Your ego's tendency to compare is more in the service of beating yourself into hopelessness."

"Why do we beat ourselves up so much?"

"All this lack of compassion, patience and love for ourselves comes from the picture our egos innocently..."

"...but misguidedly..." William interjected.

"...but misguidedly paint of perfection for ourselves – which, of course, is impossible to achieve," Charmaine asserted. "Our ego thinks if it were ever-so perfect, it would get the love it desperately needs. But it's always looking out in the world for that love."

"And it doesn't exist out there," he said.

"Right, so... we give up on ourselves. Since we can't forgive ourselves for being imperfect, we can't forgive others either."

"That makes sense. So love and respect for yourself are totally linked to loving and respecting others."

"You got it."

"Sounds like the age-old reason why people of the world can't seem to get along," said William thoughtfully.

"I'd say so," Charmaine agreed. "People of all sizes, shapes and colors give themselves a hard time. Not having affection and respect for ourselves is a first step to punishing, abusing and ultimately rejecting ourselves. And I've noticed that those who don't respect themselves have little compassion, patience, or respect for others."

"Good point," he said. "How could you love someone you don't respect?"

"And with that attitude about yourself," said Charmaine, "it's just logical you'll give others a hard time too."

"It's a vicious circle, isn't it? You know, that word 'respect' seems to come up a lot. I don't think some of the people at work give me the respect I deserve."

Charmaine hesitated. She didn't want to hurt William's feelings.

"Others tend to respect us when we respect ourselves," she said gently. "Self-respect comes from knowing who you are at a soulful level, even if you don't call it that. It's about having mercy and compassion for yourself. It's accepting all your little mistakes from the past as moments of meaning and experience to grow from. It's honoring what your feelings are there to tell you, rather than stuffing them. And perhaps most important, it's forgiving yourself for being unconscious about what you did or didn't do."

"If you feel you don't get the love and respect you deserve, William, it's usually not them but *you* who doesn't respect and love yourself."

"Ouch," William exclaimed. "I have it exactly backwards, don't I? I tend to look to others for my self-worth. I've always thought respect was tied to what I accomplish or what I own. That's not the way to look at it, huh?"

"Well, no it isn't," Charmaine agreed. "If you don't love yourself, you keep looking outside yourself for love, respect and acceptance. That kind of love is really hard to find. It's elusive, it comes and goes and is paper thin..."

"Then of course," he said, "you're also at the mercy of others – who're also unsure about who they are!"

"The only sustaining love we can ever really experience is our soul's Divine love."

"Many say that it's *God's* love we should be searching for," said William.

"Yes, and that search begins for all of us with an inward journey. Remember, William, we are all spiritual beings and we each have a soul. Our soul is our access point to the Divine. The experience of Divine love is therefore within each one of us. If we do not feel that love it is not because it is not there. It is simply because at that particular moment we are not where it is."

"Sometimes I've thought I found love out in the world," William ventured shyly.

"That's true, William, but it only lasts until your ego wants something else. It's always transient if you find it out in the world. And the only way you could find the love you're searching for out in the world, even temporarily, is because you recognize it as that same love you experience deep inside your own soul. The reality is you are actually *bringing it to* your worldly experience. It just looks like you are *finding it* out there."

"You mean like the warm, tender feeling I had when I met Emily?"

"Exactly. And that's why one good way to find love *in* the world is to realize that you are actually bringing love *to* the world."

"I'm confused. How can you find it by bringing it?"

"If you don't feel respected, be more respectful. If you don't feel like you're getting enough affection, be more affectionate. If you don't feel heard, listen more. You'll experience the very thing you're looking for by simply bringing it *to* your world."

"I think I'm starting to understand why loving yourself is so necessary."

"I know this isn't easy. Our ego keeps thinking the reason it's not getting the love it needs is either that it's not good enough or the world isn't giving it what it deserves. The problem in those moments of now is that we identify with our innocent little ego rather than with our soul."

William lowered his head, rubbing his forehead thoughtfully.

"It's not easy for me to love myself because I've been shot down, ridiculed, laughed at and questioned by my family, my teachers, my bosses and my friends most of my life. I'm going to have to look at myself differently in the future..."

"You already are, my friend. You already are. And you're doing a fine job of it too, just in case you're not in a good position to notice that."

"Thanks."

"And rest assured, you're not alone on the journey. In one way or another, we've all been treated the same way. And we all have work to do, to make ourselves whole and feel better along the way. I don't think life was set up to be a picnic for any of us. We all have our suffering to face," Charmaine assured him.

"So, how do we do that?"

"We can learn to review and reassess our previous beliefs about ourselves including what we've taken in from others. We must be willing to disregard those beliefs if they don't work for us."

"That's a mighty tall order," said William. "Holding on to old beliefs and strategies is a way of life for most of us in this corporate jungle. It is a deeply grooved habit."

"It's important to break that habit of hanging on to episodes in our lives that make us dislike ourselves. We must find compassion for those unwanted parts of ourselves, the imperfections we're afraid to look at."

"But how?"

"The first step to letting go of the past is to understand that those negative behaviors originally came out of a long-standing pattern. This 'way of being' began forming in infancy as a completely innocent strategy for love and survival. At times, it seemed to produce the results you wanted. Understanding the innocence of its origin will make it easier for you to take the second step, which is to learn to forgive yourself. That's part of the seventh Clue."

"Everything we've ever done that came from our ego's fear and sense of scarcity actually was an innocent ..." Charmaine paused and winked at her student.

"...but misguided strategy for love and survival," he answered easily.

"Our behavior often comes out of our ego's reaction to not getting what it thinks it needs or wants."

"I see myself doing that all the time," he admitted.

"And when we look into our own heart and see how confused we are, when we see our mistakes, it's not just our own mistakes we see. We also then tend to project those shortcomings on to the world around us."

"So if I don't love myself, it'll be difficult to love others."

"It's worse than that. It may be impossible to truly love at any other than an *ego level* if you don't love yourself at the *soulful level*. You see, William, the minute we reject ourselves, there is no room for love. Rejection comes from the ego's fear, not from the soul's love. So if we judge or reject others for their faults, we are effectively closing our hearts to ourselves."

"What does 'loving others' look like?

"Loving someone else is what happens when you let them be exactly who they are."

"I'm not sure I could do that!"

"Don't you want others to treat you as a unique individual and let you be who you are?"

"Well, sure..."

"Love exists when the happiness and security of another is as important to you as your own happiness and security."

"That would be easier if others wouldn't annoy me and do things that show no compassion for me," William exclaimed, looking a little alarmed.

"The answer to that is to always try to understand and be patient with others. Invariably, you'll discover that someone who rubs you the wrong way has in turn been rubbed the wrong way many times."

"Walk a mile in his shoes, huh?"

"You can also ask yourself whose voice you've been listening to. Be suspicious of the voice that always makes you right and sees others at fault. But also be suspicious of the voice that always makes you wrong and tends to defer to others."

"I know those voices well," he sighed. "Not very friendly ones at that!"

"Exactly. Try to avoid blaming others when things go wrong."

"Who'll I blame then?" William grinned sheepishly.

"No one," Charmaine laughed. "Blame is fear-based and very destructive, another soul-robbing activity. It is simply our ego's attempt to avoid letting go of being in control."

"Our ego running the show is really the biggest problem, isn't it?"

"But the good news is," said Charmaine, "you are the one that can do something to turn it around."

"How?"

"Practice opening your heart to your own closed-heartedness."

"Come again?"

"Opening your heart to your own closed-heartedness is the experience of your soul loving your ego, holding it with mercy, tenderness, compassion and patience."

"That sounds too good to be true."

"Practice being a little more gentle with yourself, William. Being gentle with yourself doesn't mean being weak or giving up who you are. It doesn't mean you never set boundaries for yourself or lose your ability to ask for what you want. And of course, you'll still know the difference between what feels right and what doesn't. You'll be amazed at the results."

"Okay, but what would loving myself look like? I mean how would I recognize it if it happened?"

"There are lots of ways you'll see it happening. For one, you'll begin to understand the difference between liking yourself and loving yourself."

"There are times when I don't like something I've done. Sometimes I don't even like who I am very much."

"That's at an ego level, William. Our ego is always judging. It likes or it dislikes. The soul always loves. Learning to practice loving yourself, that is, opening your heart to your soul's love, is healing. You'll begin to do that naturally. The soul always loves the ego. It's the ego that has difficulty allowing soulful love into its daily experience. Here's another example. Remember your feeling for George's baby?"

"Sure."

"You felt how precious he is. You respected and even felt a kind a reverence for his life, for his sweetness and innocence. Your heart couldn't help but open, William. That is because babies' hearts are naturally so open to the world. *And the power of an open heart is that a closed heart can not stay closed in its presence.* It'll either open or it will go away until it is ready to open. Words don't really do the feeling justice, do they?"

"No. They don't. I was filled with a powerful sense of awe that words just can't describe."

"Imagine holding yourself with that same feeling of love, tenderness, respect, patience and compassion."

"Oh! Oh wow, that would be amazing!"

"That's what loving yourself feels like, William. It's not ego love. It's the ego allowing the soul's love to come through. In fact, it's the same love you felt for little Jacob."

"I understand. That's a great example."

"That love comes from the same Divine source. In that space of open- heartedness, all we will see is our own and each other's innocence. In an open heart there is no fear and no judgment, just respect, tenderness and compassion. It's a very healing space. And where do you think you will find that space?" Charmaine asked with a smile.

William laughed at Charmaine's playful little quiz.

"In a moment of now! Man, it would be wonderful if I could feel about myself the way I felt about the baby." He sighed heavily. "I'm always so hard on myself. I tend to think if I'm not critical of myself, I'll never get better – I'll turn into a fat blob of do-nothing."

They laughed at the mental image.

"Charmaine, it's amazing how a newborn could make me feel that way. I'm beginning to understand why I feel a similar feeling at the waterfall and even right here at this bridge, especially at sunset. It's everywhere, isn't it? If I'm not experiencing that loving feeling, it's not because it's not there. It's because at that moment of now I am simply not where it is. If I miss that feeling, it's an indicator that my ego has taken charge. Hmm. All of a sudden that feels like a powerful and practical idea."

"It's odd," Charmaine mused, "how easy it is for me to have mercy and compassion for *your* struggle and yet sometimes have difficulty allowing that same mercy and compassion for my own struggles."

"*You* have struggles? What do you struggle with, Charmaine?"

"Oh, I have lots of struggles. Well, first of all, I struggle with some of my unhealthy habits that I just don't seem to be ready to give up. At times I get impatient with myself for smoking a cigarette now and then. I know it'd be better for me if I didn't. But I guess I just haven't quite suffered enough, to change my behavior."

"I also sometimes feel overwhelmed by all the suffering I see out in the world. It's hard to keep my heart open to it all because it pains me deeply. At times it's just too big for me. So I isolate myself from the world. Then I feel lonely."

Charmaine rubbed her sore ankle.

"I'm still not willing to stop flying as fast as I can around corners on my roller blades even though it hurts my ankle. It's been getting worse over the last few years. But I accept it as the price I pay to do something I love."

"William," Charmaine said, "there is something that helps me open my heart to myself."

"What?"

"I remind myself that *there is no premature wisdom in the universe.* In other words, we are all right on schedule in our learning process. We won't learn until we are ready to learn. Sometimes we have simply not suffered enough yet. We will keep making the same mistakes and continue to suffer until we are finally ready to let go of whatever we were holding onto. It could be an activity, a job, a relationship or a substance. For example, the short term oral comfort I get by sucking on a cigarette will feel worth it until it doesn't. That's when I will stop. Just because I think I may know what it would be wise to do, like quit smoking, does not mean I am quite ready to actually do it."

"That's a tough one to accept. It makes perfect sense but I really do think I should be further along than I am in my personal growth. I'm an adult, for crying out loud. And I'm way behind where I should be."

"Remember, William, *we're all right on schedule.* Learning life's lessons takes time. That is why it is so helpful to be patient and gentle with ourselves. We're spiritual beings doing our spiritual work while living in physical bodies in this physical world. All of us are on a journey and we'll all make it to our destinations."

"It's hard to imagine I'll ever get there. I guess it's just like our precious little egos to think we should be more evolved than we are."

"Here's a little image that may be helpful for you, William. There are two caterpillars crawling along and a butterfly flies overhead. One caterpillar turns to the other and says, 'Man, you'd never get me up in one of those!' I believe we really are all moving, some more reluctantly than others, toward an inevitable homecoming."

"What a great image. That's me all right, a reluctant traveler. I guess my little ego is just being its impatient self, expecting to be further ahead than it is."

"That's true. And that expectation shows up everywhere in our lives. Our real work is not the work we go to every day," Charmaine added. "Our jobs, our families, our communities and our world are simply the *arenas* in which we do our spiritual work."

"Now that's a whole different perspective," William said, intrigued.

"So you see," said Charmaine, "we suffer even more because we're rarely where we think we *should* be on our journey. Life's a lot easier when you give yourself permission to be exactly where you are. Remember, every moment of now is a totally fresh starting place to open your heart to yourself."

"I see what you mean. But how can I hold my heart open when I'm suffering? That's a big one for me."

"Opening your heart to your own suffering is a perfect opportunity to love yourself," she said. "Being open to fully experiencing your suffering requires a willingness, a quality of surrender. It's in that moment of your ego's willingness to let go of trying to stay in control, that it begins to let in the mercy, compassion and tenderness with which the soul holds the ego."

William still looked puzzled, so Charmaine elaborated.

"The anticipation of surrender makes the ego feel vulnerable. So unless you understand the gift of suffering, that vulnerability may keep your ego closed to the soul's love."

"One way of practicing loving yourself," she said, "is to practice going toward the places where you feel vulnerable."

"Which is totally contrary to my nature," William said with alarm. "I could get hurt!"

"That's true. I'm talking about going toward the feelings you're afraid to face. For example, when it's totally appropriate to set a boundary and say 'no' to somebody, you might not want to face your fear of disappointing them or making them mad. So you end up agreeing to things that don't feel right, thereby creating new suffering."

"Bingo," said William. "So what do you do?"

"Your willingness to go toward your feelings, to honor your own internal process, will guide you to the right choices. Your suffering, in fact, is there to tell you when you're moving in the wrong direction."

"A case of suffering being my friend," said William, nodding his understanding. "Can you give me another example of what loving myself looks like?"

"Yep. Have you ever had that feeling of 'being in the zone', William, when things just seem to flow?"

"Occasionally."

"It could be a moment of effortless activity when you're totally and joyfully absorbed. It could occur during a moment at work or play when you experience the flow of your awareness, totally present to all that's happening..."

"Such as writing, doing art, playing music or a sport?" asked William.

"Yes! In those moments of being in the zone, we tend to lose track of time. Those are the moments when the ego's incessant thinking, judging and comparing are totally absent. Not there."

"Cool."

"One of the beautiful aspects of loving yourself, then, is that in the willingness to be vulnerable and fully present, you become more authentic - the one you are when your ego's not caught up in *image management*."

"What is image management?"

"Image management has to do with the amount of time and energy your ego spends managing its image for itself and others."

"A big job!"

"I'll say! The reason your ego does this is that it doesn't trust that it is worthy of love just the way it is. On the other hand, when your heart's open to yourself, you're free of all that innocent but misguided waste of time and energy. In that space lies the possibility of intimacy with the *self*, to know and appreciate who you really are. It also opens the possibility of authentic relationships with others, to build intimate, loving connections with the world around you."

"So if I open my heart to myself I'll naturally begin to feel more compassion for others. And by opening my heart to the suffering of others, it'll help me have loving compassion for myself, at a soulful level. And so, the circle of love is complete!"

"Absolutely. Love is circular and returns to itself," Charmaine said. "And as your heart opens wider and wider you begin to feel a natural connection with all other people, even ones you don't know. You'll begin to see that each of us is like one cell in the body of humanity. At the level of the ego we're separate and alone, different and untouchable. But at the level of the soul we're literally one. We're not just *metaphorically* all connected, we're *literally* all connected. There is a soulful place inside each of us where we have that very real connection with all creatures. That's the nature of open-heartedness. *Connectedness is the very essence of Divine love.* Opening your heart to yourself, loving yourself, feeds this experience of connectedness. Again, the circle is complete."

"I like that analogy," he said. "Just the idea makes me feel relieved. I need to remember that each moment of now is a totally fresh possibility. I don't have to carry old baggage around."

"Refreshing concept, isn't it? Just try to be more accepting of yourself, of both your strengths and your weaknesses. You'll be more comfortable with your body, your thoughts and feelings."

"I'd sure spend a lot less time feeling afraid, resentful, angry, guilty and bored – wallowing in a mire of ego-driven gunk," William said, shifting uncomfortably. "Makes me tired just thinking of it!"

"I think you'll find you'll be more willing to take risks, to try new things," Charmaine added. "When you live in your passion you'll love what you do and do what you love. One of the biggest mistakes we make is to do something we don't love."

"I love my job. I just need to find a way to love my boss," William said, grinning.

"That's a good place to start. Whatever work you do, always look for ways to create real value and meaning or you'll never find the passion and energy necessary to succeed. Without passion, work becomes just one more soul-robbing activity."

"Well," William said, his excitement gaining momentum, "I *could* try some new ideas I have and maybe set bigger goals for myself. If I feel more emotionally positive, I'm sure I'll feel physically healthier, too."

"All those things," Charmaine said, laughing with delight at William's boyish excitement.

"I'm on a roll, here," he continued spiritedly. "If I'm not so hard on myself I'm sure I'd be less critical and impatient with my boss and the other people at work."

"You'd no longer confuse the mistakes you and others may make with your value as human beings." Charmaine added to William's growing list of benefits of loving himself.

"No question about it - I'm one lovable guy!"

"What's not to love?"

"Not a thing. I'm perfect," William said, giving Charmaine a hearty hug. "At a soulful level, of course..."

Finding Your Soul

Summary

Clue #4: Practice Loving Yourself

Loving yourself is embracing who you really are. It is holding yourself with tenderness and mercy. It is having compassion for yourself. It is being patient with all your shortcomings and mistakes as well as with your strengths and successes. Loving yourself opens the possibility to love others. It gives us access to feeling a sense of connectedness with the earth, all the creatures and all of humanity. Loving yourself at this soulful level is not selfish or arrogant. Loving yourself is what happens when the ego allows in the soul's Divine love.

- Loving yourself is what happens when the ego allows in the soul's Divine love.

- Loving yourself allows you to love others and receive their love in return.

- Loving yourself allows you to bring love, compassion and mercy to your world instead of trying to find love *in* it.

- The power of an open heart is that a closed heart can not stay closed in its presence. It'll either open or it will go away until it is ready to open.

- The part of us that is already perfect - our soul - loves the part of us that is not yet perfect - our ego.

- Loving yourself is opening your heart to your own closed-heartedness.

- Each moment of now is a totally fresh starting place to open your heart to yourself.

- Opening your heart to your own suffering is one of the most beautiful ways of loving yourself.

- The love we seek out in the world can only be accessed from within.

- Our ego innocently but misguidedly paints a picture of perfection that is impossible to achieve. Just choose love over fear in as many moments of now as you can.

- Loving yourself is accepting all your mistakes from the past as moments of meaning and experience from which to grow.

- If you don't feel respected, be more respectful. If you don't feel like you are getting enough affection, be more affectionate. If you don't feel heard, listen more.

- Review and reassess your previous beliefs about yourself and the world around you. Be willing to disregard them if they don't work.

- Be a witness to your thoughts so you can be fair to yourself. Dismantle the patterns of thinking that have kept love and true happiness away. Be suspicious of the voice that always makes you right or always makes you wrong.

- Comparing yourself to others is rarely in service to loving yourself.

- There is no premature wisdom in the universe. We are all right on schedule. So be gentle with yourself.

At Work

- Never confuse your mistakes in your job with your value as a human being.

- If you don't love your work or don't try to find ways to have real value and meaning in what you do, then you will never find the energy and passion that is necessary to succeed.

The Benefits of Understanding Loving Yourself

Loving yourself allows you to know and appreciate who you really are. It opens the possibility of having authentic relationships with others and intimate connections with the world around you. By loving yourself you will be more willing to take on bigger games and challenges.

Exercise

Opening Your Heart To Yourself

This exercise will help you get in touch with the experience of loving yourself. You will then be better able to look at yourself with tenderness and compassion.

Being sensitive to the gender issue, we've decided to interchange male and female pronouns in each step. If you are a woman, we invite you to read all of them as she or her. If you are a man we invite you to read them as he or him.

Step 1: Sit quietly, close your eyes and take a few softening breaths.

Step 2: Begin to scan back through the images and memories of an earlier time in your life. Be a loving witness to whatever arises in your mind. Go back to high school. Recall where you lived, people you spent time with, places you went. Go back further. Recall grade school. Again, recall the activities and people, and remember the places where you spent time.

Step 3: Now recall a moment from your early childhood when your feelings were hurt. Get a clear image of the situation. In your mind's eye, take yourself back to that moment of the hurt feelings. Notice the time of day that it occurred. Notice where you were, who was there and what was happening. Let the feelings of hurt, disappointment or fear into your awareness. Feel them as completely as you can.

Step 4: Notice what it feels like to need to be loved, to feel safe and happy and notice what it feels like not to get those things. Let yourself feel the sadness and the loneliness and remember the scared feelings. Whatever you needed in that moment, let yourself feel what it was like *not* to get it.

Step 5: Now step back in your mind's eye and let yourself feel sadness and compassion for that little child who was being hurt in some way. Imagine going to that little child in you and taking him out of that bad situation. Take him to a place where he feels safe. Now pick him up and put your arms around him and let him feel your love, your strength and you calmness. Let yourself feel how good it feels to hold him and to love him.

Nobody knows or understands his pain like you do. You are the only one that truly understands what he feels and what he really needs. Whatever it is take care of it. If he's hungry - feed him. If he's cold - make him warm. If he's lonely - play with him. If he needs to cry, invite him to cry just as long and as hard and as deeply as he can. Your job is simply to keep holding him and loving him.

Step 6: Now notice how good it feels to you to open your heart to her. Let yourself love her.

Step 7: Ask him how he's doing. When he feels safe and comfortable, let him know that your love for him is absolute and unconditional. Reassure him that it never matters what he ever does or does not do, that you will always love him. Let him know that you will always come to him if he needs you. Tell him that all he has to do is to call you and you'll come to him just as quickly as you can.

Step 8: When all that is done and she feels safe and loved, step back, gently hold her hands and look into her eyes. Now reassure her one more time that your love is absolute and unconditional. Let her know all she has to do is to call you and you will come to her.

Step 9: You will know the little child in you needs you when you start feeling that pain. That scary, bad, lonely or hurt feeling *is* the little boy in you calling you. At that moment you now begin to have a choice. You can either be that child, stuck in his hurt, loneliness and fear, or you can learn to step back, open your heart and take care of him.

Step 10: Now find a photograph of yourself at about that age. Make several copies of it and have them around in different places in your life, at home, at work and wherever you're alone. Look at that picture often, especially for the first few weeks. As you look at it let yourself feel the love and compassion you feel for that wonderful little child. See her innocence. Your job is to develop a loving, respectful, tender and helpful relationship with her. It is your job in life to learn how to recognize when she needs you and to learn to go to her, to love her and to be effective in taking care of her.

If you don't have a photo of yourself at that age, find or create some object that reminds you of her. It could be a picture of a little dog, a baseball mitt, a doll, a piece of jewelry, a stuffed animal - anything that helps you get the feeling of opening your heart to that little child who will always be with you. Remember, there is nothing wrong with who that child is. It is simply that at that age she was not as effective as you can now be at taking care of her.

Principle

Learning to open your heart to yourself as a child, a teenager or as an adult is a profound and very practical way to identify with your soul rather than your ego and will allow you to open your heart to the rest of the world.

Chapter Seven

Clue # 5

Be Honest With Yourself in All Things.

It was another glorious sunny afternoon. Charmaine roller-bladed to the park to meet William, refreshed by her routine of meditation and workout. From his general appearance, Charmaine surmised he was feeling quite a bit better about his life. He looked happy, alert and pleased to be alive.

"How are you feeling today?" she asked, sitting next to him on the bench.

"Hey, Charmaine! I feel good... as a matter of fact, I... feel... f-f-fantas... fantas... tic...," William exclaimed.

A tear – clearly a tear of joy – welled up in William's eye. His emotions seemed to teeter right on the surface.

"Sorry," he said, startled by this unexpected display. "Oh, man, this is awkward... it's j-j-just that I f-feel so relieved."

"You needn't apologize," Charmaine said, patting his arm. "Your feelings are real, so it's good for you to express them. "

"Maybe, but not *here*... not in front of *people*!"

"Why not?" she asked lightly. "You're sharing with me the truth about who you really are and what's going on inside you in this moment of now."

"I think I'd rather do that and skip the tears," William said, unconvinced.

"In some of our most radical moments of honesty, people often cry. I've always thought of crying as a natural storm flowing through us. It's a release that freshens and invigorates us as it passes by. Crying is normal, even healthy, William."

"Not for guys."

"Sure it is. Tears are nature's way to help you release strong feelings of sadness and grief. On the other hand, they can also express great relief or even joy. Remember, you can think of feelings as *emotional gas,*" she chuckled.

William laughed. "Want to hear some?"

"Only if it's an honest expression of your feelings," Charmaine said with a grin. "You know," she continued more seriously, "feelings really are about honesty. Times when we cry are some of our more honest moments we have with ourselves. To do that in the presence of another is very intimate."

"Yeah, more intimate than I'm comfortable with! I've always thought that crying, especially in front of another person, is a sign of weakness."

"Not at all," she exclaimed. "Crying actually reflects inner strength and honesty. It shows *inner strength* because it requires a clear intention and willingness to stay present to those kinds of intense feelings. Crying shows *honesty* because it reflects a willingness to face what is actually going on deep inside you. It takes courage to be honest, William."

"I suppose so," he said, pondering her words.

"There are two kinds of honesty: honesty with yourself and honesty with others. If you're not honest with yourself it's tough to be honest with others. Lying to others is the logical by-product of lying to yourself."

"It would have to be, wouldn't it," William agreed thoughtfully.

"No question about it," she answered. "Being honest with yourself requires courage and a healthy skepticism toward your old beliefs and assumptions."

"But my beliefs are important to me. You know, sometimes it feels as if I need to be right."

"We can learn to let go of *needing* to be right, William. The greatest obstacle to discovering truth is being convinced you already know it."

"Hmmm. Good point."

"We all tend to think we're objective, that we see things as they really are..."

"...but reality is what it is," said William.

"Our ego doesn't even have access to 'reality' except through its own frame of reference, which is made up of our unseen thoughts -

attitudes, beliefs and assumptions. The only legitimate question is, 'Would you like to know the frame of reference through which your ego tends to view reality?' Imagine looking at life through a window which is gray and critical. So everywhere you look, everything looks a little gray, and you see lots to criticize."

"Charmaine, it would be like looking through a pair of sunglasses, wouldn't it? Everything you see is affected by the lens and after a while, you think that's the way it really is."

"Nice illustration, William, but it's actually more like you're looking at life through a pair of extended-wear soft contact lenses that you forgot you had in. And since the universe is wired up to provide us with evidence that supports whatever position we've already taken about life, we can't even test it out. So if you think your boss is a jerk, you will see evidence to support that. If you think Emily is beautiful, you will see her beauty. If you think you can't do something, guess what? You can't do it. You can't test it out if you can't see that how you experience your life is based not on reality, but rather on the lens of the window you don't even know you're looking through."

"I've been seeing life through a more rosy, appreciative window lately. Does that mean I'm just making it all up?"

"Yes."

"Yes?"

Charmaine laughed. "That's what we all do! It's natural," she said. "Again, the question is, 'Would you like to know about the lens through which you've been looking at the world?' The quality of the *lens* through which we experience life is made up of our unseen thoughts, attitudes and beliefs. Too often we blindly accept what we're told by others, who may or may not be well-intentioned. Our perceptions are so colored by the stories we tell ourselves of our past experiences, we often get stuck and miss the truth about ourselves. It's important to have the courage and self-respect to keep taking a fresh look at ourselves with integrity and compassion. Don't forget compassion."

"Well, I think it would be really hard to separate my *assumptions* about truth from truth itself," said William.

"You're right. It *is* difficult," Charmaine agreed. "One of the best ways to find the truth within you, though, is to notice how your body reacts to what you're thinking."

"Now, I think I could do that!"

"Those uncomfortable feelings are there to tell you whether or not you're being honest with yourself. An upset stomach, tightness in your chest or a headache can be symptoms that let you know you need an internal reality-check. Anger, irritation, resistance and fear indicate that you may be having problems."

"Problems with what?"

"With facing the truth, or accepting the fact that you need to make a change in your life, or your approach to life," said Charmaine. "It's also possible to feel similar physical reactions when *others* are dishonest with you."

"Like the feeling you get when you know someone is lying or trying to mislead you?"

"You feel uncomfortable and off-balance, don't you," she asked, nodding in agreement. "And you probably experience negative emotions as well as a physical reaction towards them, too."

"Yes, I do! That must be why I feel so irritable around a few people at work who seem like such phonies."

"I imagine so. And the same thing happens when you know you're lying to yourself. When you try to hide aspects of yourself or your behavior, your shame seems to grow. It distances you from others. You cut yourself off from real help. Sometimes, when it's tough to find clarity, we might need help from outside ourselves. It can be helpful to talk to friends, your mate, or your co-workers and ask what they think when you're struggling."

"I don't know. That sounds risky."

Charmaine shrugged. "If you can't speak the truth to someone else, it's not a relationship; it's an arrangement, a charade, a dance between two facades."

"But they might not understand," William said with a worried expression.

"Or they may see you more clearly than you see yourself," Charmaine suggested. "We're always more transparent than we think. People can see right through our image-management, if they're paying any attention at all. Remember, the reason to tell the truth is not so much for the benefit of others but for us to feel authentic and real to ourselves. When you're true to yourself, you feel more alive."

"Okay," William replied with a smirk and a wink, "but I'm not going to ask that long-haired salesman, John, how he sees me. I think he set his hair dryer on stun once too often. He must have fried a few brain neurons."

Charmaine laughed with William and squeezed his arm affectionately. William's true personality seemed to be re-emerging, sense of humor and all! 'Good!' she thought contentedly, and drew a deep breath of fresh air.

After a few moments of silence, Charmaine turned to William and looked him straight in the eye.

"Your truth is your power. It allows access to your clarity, and clarity wields its own power. Honesty can also be your salvation, because it will save you from a world of problems, guiding you out of countless messes."

"But honesty," she continued, "may also create some of its own problems. In the long run, though, it will serve you better than lies. Once you understand that and believe it, life gets simpler and more joyous."

"Sometimes it's so uncomfortable to be honest," William said, shuddering a little.

"It's usually the *anticipation* of telling the truth that's so scary for our ego," she answered. "My father once said, 'When you're with someone and you realize there is something you're afraid to say, it's probably the first thing you need to say.' I would add, '…if you can do it with an open heart.'"

"Being honest with yourself and the world around you will also guide you to your life purpose. The more honest you are with yourself, the more you'll know and understand who you are. Thus the more passion and aliveness you'll feel."

"I'm for more passion and aliveness," William grinned playfully. "Honest!"

"That's the spirit," Charmaine grinned. "Your journey has already begun, and honesty is like a compass on that journey. You'll know when you're on track because life feels energizing and clear. If you get off course, you'll know that too, because something won't feel right. And the added benefit when you tell the truth is that you don't have to remember everything you said!" Now Charmaine grinned playfully. "That's a big plus when you get as old as I am."

"What if I make mistakes …?"

"If you start looking at yourself with the love and compassion you so richly deserve, you'll soon realize that *there are no real mistakes, only lessons.*"

"No mistakes," William repeated. *No mistakes?*"

"Pleasant thought, isn't it?" Charmaine smiled at her friend's expression of incredulity. "It doesn't serve you to stay upset with yourself. Just pay attention to how you behaved, learn the lesson and gently move on. Be patient with yourself the way you were with the world when you were first in love. We're all 'in process'. So who we are *inside* and what we do on the *outside* will not always be aligned. All of life is a growth process. Stumbling and falling sometimes is a natural part of the journey."

"That's reassuring," William sighed.

"When people understand the power of being honest with themselves, they gain clarity. They can tell their truth because there's nothing left to fear."

"Nothing left to fear," William reflected. "Wouldn't *that* be heaven!"

"Wouldn't it," Charmaine agreed wholeheartedly. "In the process, you develop love and compassion for yourself. And here's the bonus: you then create an intimate connection and caring for others."

"I'm going to practice being honest with myself," William resolved. "It sure seems worth it to make the effort. What about honesty with others? Why *do* we lie so much?"

"That's a really significant question. We're born with basic emotional needs. We need totally unconditional love absolutely guaranteed in each and every moment of now throughout our entire lives. But our ego thinks it has to do something to get that love. It believes we are clearly not good enough - deficient in some way - or we would be getting that love. So we begin, even in infancy to develop a *way of being* in the world. This way of being is designed to increase the likelihood of getting the love we need and want. It's also designed to help us deal with the pain of not getting that love. This is the beginning of our lying, or our *image management.* It's part of our ego's innocent but misguided strategy for finding the love it wants."

"The chances of getting the love we really need and want look pretty bleak."

"That's true, William, as long as you're looking out in the world for it."

"That's what the inward journey is all about, isn't it?"

"Yes. Remember, at a soulful level, through an inward journey, *we all have access to infinite love!* We have Divine access to exactly what our ego so desperately searches for out in the world. And when you learn to tap into that infinite and unconditional love, you can first bring it to your starving ego. Then you can bring that same quality of joy, well-being and love *to* your life, your work, your relationships and your world instead of running around trying to find love in your world."

"I had never thought about bringing love to the world, rather than seeking love from the world," he said. "Imagine if everyone did that!"

Charmaine closed her eyes and visualized a world like that. She breathed deeply and opened her eyes to William.

"Yes, imagine! The beauty of honesty is that the more truthful you are, the more you're aligned with your authentic self, your soul."

"So, honesty," William concluded, "is an access point to infinite love."

"That's been my experience," she said warmly.

"Would you say honesty is an access key to the quality of life?"

"It can be. But not being totally enlightened, we're unlikely to be in that space all the time. It *is* possible, though, to cultivate *defenselessness* and *telling on yourself,* practices which help make that happen in more moments of now than you might imagine."

"What do you mean by practicing defenselessness and telling on yourself?" William asked.

"Your ego is the only thing that ever needs defending," Charmaine explained. "On the other hand, your soul is infinitely safe. So if someone criticizes you, try looking for the kernel of truth in their accusation. Acknowledge it rather than respond to the part that may not feel true."

William shifted uneasily.

"Telling on yourself," she continued, noting William's discomfort, "is volunteering information that your ego would be defensive about. The anticipation of this gives your ego the willies, but it's a wonderful way to get out of your ego and back to your soul. Telling on yourself is an extension of practicing defenselessness."

"Can you give me an example?"

"Sure, William. Before I told you about my smoking I realized a part of me did not want you to know that. I thought you might think badly of me or that I would lose credibility with you. But after I mentioned it I felt relieved that I had been honest and not hidden anything from you. Otherwise I would have felt like I was living a lie with you."

"Charmaine, I have to admit when you told me about your smoking, all of a sudden I felt closer to you. It felt good. Like maybe I don't have to be perfect either. A strong argument for honesty," said William.

"Yes, I felt closer to you too. Another major aspect of our 'way of being' in the world is that most people have a very low tolerance for conflict and disharmony."

"That's me," William said. "I'll do almost anything to avoid it."

"Which usually leads to a lie, right?"

"Well, I try not to lie..."

"When we say 'yes' to things that don't feel right, to avoid hurting someone's feelings or disappointing them, that's a lie."

"Well. In that case, I guess I'm a *prolific* liar," William exclaimed.

"Withholding love and support out of fear or resentment is just as much a lie as giving more than is healthy to give."

"I remember lying to my parents because I didn't want to disappoint them," said William thoughtfully.

"Yes, unfortunately, lying is one of the first things we learn to do. Our parents and others around us unwittingly reinforce it."

"And at work," William added, "I say things I don't really mean, to protect a co-worker or make someone feel better."

"We tell ourselves we lie because we don't want to hurt someone else's feelings. But generally it's ourselves we're protecting. We don't want to feel what we feel when we see someone we care about suffering."

"I hadn't thought of it that way," said William. "Now that I think about it, I guess I do sort of lie to help interactions go smoother, and to protect myself from embarrassment and disapproval. Or to get myself out of a bind."

Charmaine sighed. "Our tendency to not tell the truth is pervasive, isn't it? We lie to make ourselves look better, to make a positive impression on others and even to gain advantage over someone else. There seems no end to the reasons we won't allow ourselves to just tell the truth!"

"I suppose because lying so often feels like the kinder thing to do," he said.

"Not in the long-run," she assured him. "When we lie, we lose our necessary, appropriate and healthy boundaries. A wise old friend of mine calls this a *disease of chronic self-neglect*."

"Lying is a form of self-neglect?"

"Yes, when we become *preoccupied* with what others feel, need and want," Charmaine answered. "If we do this long enough, we lose sight of who we really are and what we really feel and what we really need and want."

"Oh, okay, I see what you're getting at," William said.

"It's also a part of that innocent but misguided strategy for love and survival. It's misguided because there is no amount of anything we could ever *do*, anything we could ever *have* or anything we could ever *be* that would actually cause us to get the love we need. The physical world of reality simply doesn't offer it in that size package. But it's the only place our ego knows to look."

"You know, Charmaine, some lies don't seem so bad. Like white lies - they seem harmless and are done out of kindness, aren't they?"

"I suppose if you're consciously aware that you're lying and know you want to do it, you might be able to live with yourself," Charmaine admitted cautiously. "But you're just lying to get through the moment. Unfortunately, by making lying a lifestyle, you miss the moment. And you miss the next moment. Lying cuts off your access to being fully present in a moment of now."

"I suppose most people opt for the easy way out of a difficult situation," he said.

"People obviously believe that lying makes life easier. But when lies mount up, we get stressed and we don't feel good. In the end, we're confused and inauthentic."

"Not to mention 'wrong'," he added.

"Being honest is *practical*. If you live a lie, eventually your life won't work. If you tell the truth, especially with grace and love, you'll feel better - and just be happier."

"I know," interjected William, "but telling the bare-naked truth is hard because it goes against our conditioning. Being polite to avoid telling the truth, being tactful and for that matter, being politically correct at the expense of telling the truth, is constantly reinforced by our whole society."

"True," said Charmaine.

"Maybe it's all right for poker players and actors to lie, but I frankly feel betrayed when politicians and some of our business leaders lie for the sake of greed and power," he said, gathering momentum.

"I don't think there is anything inherently wrong with business or capitalism. I know business can be done ethically and produce a quality product and still make a reasonable profit without exploitation. But I'm constantly being bombarded with advertising that's barely truthful! Then there are the offers I get from credit card companies and banks, barely readable contracts printed in the smallest of type. And what about those increasingly complicated phone bills. The way they present those bills, you'd almost have to be an attorney to understand them..."

Charmaine paused to let William catch his breath. "You're right," she said with a smile. "Those things don't reflect much honesty."

"If lying doesn't 'pay', I'm sure not seeing evidence of it in the everyday business world. On the contrary. It seems to pay big!"

"It may not always appear to 'cost' in the short term," she said, "but it eventually does exact a price, William, both in the bottom line and spiritually. Lying is a *soul-robbing activity.*"

"Wow, you can say *that* again!"

"Lying is a soul-robbing activity, William," Charmaine repeated solemnly. It also affects one's health more than most people might think. It can cause insomnia and other physical problems. Let's face it, the stress of constantly pretending and avoiding being found out, and the wear and tear of misleading others, is an ongoing source of misery. Telling the truth can actually relieve feelings of depression and anxiety. Without honesty we can't move on. We just stay stuck."

"And people don't trust liars!" he added.

"Most people see right through a lie if they're paying any attention at all," Charmaine agreed. "Think of it this way, William. Imagine a magic hat. When you wear this hat everyone within five hundred feet of you knows every thought you have. To the degree you're willing to wear this magic hat, you're a free person. And in order to wear this magic hat, you really have to trust in yourself and the rest of the world. Trust is the most essential ingredient to real success and meaningful relationships."

"I was just thinking of that wonderful movie, *Forrest Gump*. Gump was so likable partly because he could *only* tell the truth, and it always worked out for him."

"I liked that movie, too. Gump showed us that honesty leads to stronger and more loving relationships. When people tell the truth about who they are, what they've done, what they feel and what they're thinking, they have nothing to hide. They find a new kind of freedom."

William put out his hand to help Charmaine up.

"I'd give anything to be that kind of free," he said finally.

"In that case," said Charmaine quietly, "you're on the right path."

Summary

Clue #5
Be Honest With Yourself in All Things.

The power of honesty is that the more you tell the truth to yourself and the world around you, the more you are aligned with your authentic self, your soul. Though we are all quite transparent, the reason for telling the truth is not so much for others as for our own benefit. With it comes a feeling of aliveness, authenticity and new life-energy. All honesty begins with honesty with yourself.

- Honesty is an access point to infinite love.

- There are two kinds of honesty: honesty with yourself and honesty with others.

- If you're honest with yourself it's easier to be honest with others.

- Telling the truth is contrary to our early conditioning.

- Withholding our love and support from others out of fear and resentment is just as much a lie as giving more than is healthy for us to give.

- Being honest with yourself requires courage and a healthy skepticism toward your old beliefs.

- The greatest obstacle to discovering the truth is being convinced you already know it.

- Our physical reactions can indicate whether we are telling the truth.

- The more you are honest with yourself, the more you will know yourself and understand who you are.

- We are always more transparent than we think. The power of honesty is this: the more you tell the truth to yourself and the world around you, the more you are aligned with your authentic self, your soul.

- We often are dishonest because we have a very low tolerance for conflict and disharmony.

- We often lie to protect ourselves and others from consequences, punishment, embarrassment and disapproval, or to 'look good' and gain advantage over others.

- Lying is a sympton of the disease of chronic self-neglect.

- Lying is soul-robbing and it affects our mental and physical health.

- If you lie you won't trust others and they won't trust you.

- If you live a lie your life won't work.

At Work

- If you can't speak the truth to others, it's not a relationship - it's a charade.

- Being honest with yourself and the world around you will help guide you to your life purpose.

- If you live a lie at work, eventually your private life won't work either.

The Benefits of Being Honest With Yourself

Telling the truth can relieve depression, anxiety, insomnia, physical illness and the stress of constantly pretending. In the process of telling the truth, you develop love and compassion for yourself. And here's the bonus: you then create the possibility of an intimate connection and concern for others.

Exercise

"Death Bed Analysis"

Step 1: Find a comfortable, quiet, warm place to lie down. Make yourself as comfortable as possible. Take a few softening breaths and close your eyes. Decide to relax and let go of any concerns for the next 15 minutes.

Step 2: Now imagine yourself on your death bed. Find someplace that feels safe and comfortable. Imagine peacefully lying down gazing out on a sunset. Now reflect back on your life and begin to ask yourself some questions . You will find you are much clearer about things if you project yourself forward to your death bed and look back at your life as a whole experience. Ask questions such as: "Did I spend too much time watching TV, not enough time or just the right amount?" "Did I spend too much time listening to the children, not enough time or just the right amount?" "Did I get too many massages, not enough massages or just the right amount?"

Step 3: Now ask yourself a more difficult question about something that has been on your mind lately. Again, project yourself forward and then look back seeing your life as one whole experience. Ask a question such as: "Should I have gone back to school or was it really too late?" "Should I have stayed at that job?" "Should I have taken that vacation?" "Could I have more fully committed to my relationship? What would that have looked like?"

Principle

The clarity you can find in this exercise will help you take action in any arena of your life. Projecting yourself into the future and looking back can sometimes take you to the place where your clarity is waiting. Clarity has its own power. This is useful way to be honest with yourself without all the distractions, considerations, image management and concerns of your daily life. Being honest with yourself, coming from a deep clarity, empowers you to be honest with others and to take the steps necessary to align your current life patterns with your deeper values.

Chapter Eight

Clue #6

Let Go of Attachment to Outcome.

On his walk home from work, William had begun stopping to exchange pleasant conversation with his neighbors as he passed. One afternoon he stopped to chat with his friend George and his wife Irene.

"Hey, I just wanted to thank both of you for a great party last weekend!"

"Hi, William," George called from the driveway where he was washing his car.

Irene was trimming a rose bush. "Glad you came!", she said. "You sure made a hit with the baby. Jacob doesn't let just *anybody* hold him..."

"He's such a great kid," William said, recalling Jacob's sweet smile. He had felt better just being around the little guy. "He's such a smile magnet! Everybody just lights up around him."

"That's my boy, all right," George said affectionately.

"Anyway, I sure had a good time. I didn't know anybody could have that many friends and family! And all so friendly!"

"Yeah, we're pretty blessed, William," agreed George. "But don't wait for a party to visit us – you're always welcome."

"Thanks! I haven't reached out to others over the last few years, but I've started to lately, and it feels good. "

"Hey, my cousin Howard said you were the star of the softball game - said he'd never seen anybody hit the ball as far as you did, a grand-slam home run at that."

William smiled modestly, pleased with the compliment.

"Tell me, George, isn't it hard to have all these people in your life, especially Jacob, without always worrying about their safety? I mean, it really is a jungle out there, and you can't control all the bad things that could happen to your loved ones."

"William, I believe we all have good instincts, and it's wise to pay attention to them, to trust all our senses. But that's not the same as worrying all the time. There are things we simply have no control over. If I spent all my time being anxious about what *could* happen," George said with a chuckle, "I'd probably miss what *is* happening."

"True," said William thoughtfully.

"We all love each other and I figure people are doing pretty much the best they can. Most things seem to work out fairly well most of the time, don't you think?"

"I'd *like* to think that," William said wistfully.

"Now I admit, sometimes awful things happen," said George. "Last year, for example, a drunk driver killed my nephew on his way home from a soccer tournament. It was very traumatic for the whole family."

"How terrible! Didn't you just hate the guy that did that?"

"We *were* angry and *very sad.*"

"I can imagine," William exclaimed sympathetically.

"We grieved... deeply. Then we talked about the accident, to see if there was anything we could learn from it. And finally we were able to begin letting go of the tragedy and go on with our lives."

"But it's so hard!"

"I can't even *tell* you how hard," George sighed. "But that's just the way it is. We won't allow life's brutal side to rob us of our joy."

"You're starting to sound a lot like my friend Charmaine."

George laughed.

"Actually, Charmaine shared the Clues with my father years ago. We've all passed down that ancient wisdom as best we can. She's been a friend of our family as long as anyone can remember."

"She never told me that. I *wondered* why so many people at the party already knew her. She's a good friend to me, too – and a real help. That Charmaine is a mysterious and fascinating woman," William said chuckling. "It's hard to imagine she's that old. Sometimes she seems like a young woman and at other times she has such an *ancient presence.*"

"That's our Charmaine, all right," Irene said, smiling.

William said good-bye to George and Irene and walked several more blocks past his place toward the zoo. As he walked, he thought about what George had said.

"If I let go of caring about outcomes," he thought to himself, "I'm afraid I'd be a sitting duck for all the advantage-takers in my life." William smiled wryly at the bizarre notion of a duck sitting on a stool, with *his* head attached.

Soon he spotted Charmaine waiting at the entrance gate of the zoo, where they'd agreed to meet.

"Good afternoon my power-hitting friend."

"Hi, Charmaine." William smiled a proud little boy kind of smile.

"I just stopped by George's place. Why didn't you tell me you knew his family and had also coached them over the years? I know a guy isn't supposed to ask a woman a question like this but exactly how old are you, Charmaine?"

"Age is relative, William," she said with a 'you're right, don't ask' smile. "As for George's family, it wasn't my intention to mislead you. It just didn't seem important at the time. Besides," she grinned, "you were having so much fun introducing me to everyone. You were right, though, about the new baby. Little Jacob is truly a precious child. Just imagine what it would be like if we all could see that innocence not only in ourselves but in everyone we meet!"

William laughed.

"It's probably hard to see because most people don't seem that innocent."

"It's there in all of us even if we don't see it," Charmaine said softly.

"It would be a life-changing miracle if I could feel that way about everyone," he said.

"Just remember, William, all that really exists in life are moments of now. Each one is a fresh possibility to open your heart and see that innocence. You can see the innocence of others without giving up the ability to ask for what you want, or the right to say *no*, and generally, to take exquisite care of yourself. You just need to be willing and able to set healthy boundaries."

"I guess that does make sense," he admitted. "It sure is easy to set yourself up for failure even when your intentions are good, isn't it? I've been struggling with something lately. Maybe you can help me out."

"I'll do my best."

"There's been a lot of pressure at work around a big contract we're trying to land. It's really important to our company. All the mucky-mucks are sticking their noses into everything. Sometimes I have trouble getting to sleep. I wake up in the middle of the night worrying and can't get back to sleep. It's awful. When I come home from work lately I feel tired, anxious, frustrated and unsure about some of the decisions I've made."

Charmaine had seen this problem with many people lately. With all the new technology, the pace of life seems to move faster than most folks can keep up with.

"William, you have a choice about how you feel at work - and after you come home from work."

"How's that?"

"I think it's time for us to talk about the sixth Clue: practicing *letting go of attachment to outcome*. It's a big one, but it can totally change how you experience your life. Let's walk; there's something I want to show you.

As they strolled past the camels and ostriches, William talked about how hard it was to do his best when he worried so much about how things would turn out, especially at work.

"I worry myself sick wondering if my work will please the boss and whether our company will get that big contract. How can I let go of my attachment to that outcome? My job might depend on it. Everybody is uptight about it, which is normal..."

"No, it is not *normal*," said Charmaine. "It's just very *common*. Do the best you can, because after that point the results are out of your hands, anyway. And like most people, if things go your way you'll want to take credit. But if things don't go well, you'll probably feel guilty and depressed, and try to determine who's fault it is. Neither of these options is healthy or necessary."

They approached the primate section and Charmaine stopped. A beautiful old tree grew at the center. It was immense, towering over the other trees. Its lofty branches extended over a rugged terrain far below.

"William, what do you see?"

He looked at the magnificence of the setting. It seemed bigger than life and exquisitely beautiful. He saw this one gigantic tree mingling its branches and limbs with the other trees that formed the lush green covering. He noticed the canopy far above as the wind blew the tops of the trees. The branches swayed far over in one direction and then back to the other side as if riding a strong tide of air. They were always in motion.

William heard the sounds of birds, melodious and sweet as he noticed sunlight streaming through the treetops. Then he noticed the monkeys. Lots of them! They leapt and swung all over the place, apparently playing monkey-tag. Others just seemed to be swinging around because they could. They jumped from branch to branch, from tree to tree. Their playful antics looked effortless.

"This is pretty amazing," he said to Charmaine. "I've never seen so many monkeys all at once. They seem to be having a great time."

"Yes, they do. How far down do you think it is from where those monkeys are jumping around?"

"I don't know ... a hundred feet. Maybe more. Why?"

"What do you suppose would happen if one failed to catch hold of the branch it was reaching for?"

"It'd fall and certainly be killed," William said with a shudder.

"Nonetheless, they don't seem too worried about it, do they?"

"Okay, I see," said William, nodding. "They've learned to let go of their attachment to the outcome of each and every leap, so they're much more effective and successful at leaping."

"You've got it! Letting go of attachment to outcome doesn't mean you don't care about it..."

"...attachment to the outcome," William broke in enthusiastically, "is just a fear-based distraction to being fully present and available to do your best! Whew, what a revolutionary concept."

"You see," Charmaine added, "the soul has no attachments. Only our ego forms attachments."

"And those attachments are the source of *all* our suffering," William said, putting the pieces together.

"It's very difficult for the ego to just let go," she said. "Remember, the ego thinks ..."

"... its survival depends on being in control," William said, finishing the sentence.

"Good. You remembered. The soul is naturally *connected* to everything around us. On the other hand, the ego tends to get *enmeshed and entangled* with its surroundings. Being *connected* and being *attached* are not the same."

"So, being unattached to outcome," William said, "means that my happiness, safety and security don't depend on the outcome! And my happiness, safety and security are always present at that core level of my soul."

"You're right, William. Being fully present in the moment allows you to experience the soul's natural connection with the world around you. In that space, you're not worrying about what might or might not happen next."

William spoke under his breath as if trying to internalize the concept by consciously repeating it.

"The soul's natural *connection* with life is very different from the ego's *attachments* in life."

"Yes. Attachment is a form of addiction," Charmaine added. "And like all addictions, attachments spring from our ego and are designed to serve two purposes. One is to help us *avoid a feeling* we are afraid to face, and the other is to artificially *create a feeling, like with alcohol or drugs*, that our ego can't seem to create on its own."

Charmaine gestured toward the monkeys darting about in the trees.

"These monkeys have no attachment to outcome. Their life depends on being successful. And like your life - and especially your job - the monkey's goal is a moving target."

"You can say that again! I get dizzy just watching them hurtling about."

"How do you suppose they let go and just *go for it* all the time?"

"Beats me!"

"It's because they're fully present," she continued, "and have a natural sense of connection with their environment. It's in this state of awareness, connection and being fully present that we are most effective in all the things that we do. This includes your job, William."

"Being fully present is usually difficult when I'm at work," he sighed.

"That's a common experience but it doesn't need to be true. There's a reason we're most effective in all things when we come from our soulful place of non-attachment. It's the only place where we have access to our timing, our balance, our discernment, our intuition, our creativity, our power, our passion - all the things that our soul provides. None of those qualities has its source in our ego."

"These monkeys are a great illustration for being fully present in moments of now," William said with a chuckle. "I'd have never guessed I could learn such a profound lesson from a bunch of monkeys!"

"That's part of the beauty of living in this world, isn't it," Charmaine said with a touch of humor. "Certain creatures have an easier time with some of the Clues than others. It's part of the Mystery of life. But we're all here to help each other discover whatever we need to learn next."

"Learning to let go of my attachments to outcome would definitely make my life easier, I agree, but unlike Mr. Monkey, I find it a pretty tough thing to do."

"Yes it is. But, guess what? You naturally spend more time in that free state of being than you may realize."

"That's encouraging. How?"

"Do you recall the softball game last Saturday, when you hit the home run and knocked in the winning runs?"

"How could I forget? I was in sports-heaven!"

"Do you remember being attached to the outcome in the moment of now when you hit the ball?"

"No, of course not." William puffed out his chest in a playful display of machismo. "I was just gettin' it done! I mean I was like floatin' - in the *zone!*"

Charmaine smiled at his silliness. She enjoyed seeing William loosening up.

"But you're right," he said. "I wasn't worrying about anything. It was effortless, energizing and pure joy. I was just there, as you would say, *fully present*, not thinking about anything – certainly not the future or the past. I just knew intuitively exactly when to swing at the ball." William grinned. "I smashed it in a major way. It *was* a beauty, wasn't it?"

"You were magnificent," she agreed. "That's what it's like when you let go of *attachment* to outcome. You naturally produce your best outcome."

"That's so simple, it's profound. By the way, Charmaine, did you notice the woman sitting with George and Irene - the one cheering me on?"

"Yes, I did," she said with a twinkle in her eye.

"That's my new friend, Emily, but I suppose you already know that," he said giving her arm an affectionate 'buddy' punch.

"I'm Emily's godmother," Charmaine admitted with a conspiratorial grin.

"Surprise, surprise," William said. "Anyway, I have to admit I did notice her noticing me. But at those moments when I was rounding the bases, I wasn't worried about what she might think. I might have," he added thoughtfully," if I'd slipped and fallen when I took that fast turn around second base..."

"But you didn't. Perhaps the reason you didn't fall, the reason you were in balance and your timing at the plate was perfect, is precisely because in those moments of now you weren't attached to outcome and totally present.

"Like the monkeys."

"Yes, like the monkeys. Try turning up your awareness and begin noticing those moments when you are naturally free of attachments."

"Uh, how difficult is it to count to one!" William laughed good-naturedly at himself.

"There are more of those moments than you would guess," Charmaine said. "And also notice those moments when you're entangled in your thoughts and attachments. Without judgment, just start to lovingly notice. *Be* the loving witness within. You'll gradually begin to see such an amazing difference that you will naturally start practicing letting go of attachments."

"I like that idea, Charmaine. But tell me more about what you mean by *attachments*."

"People form attachments all the time. We can get attached to anything, like objects, other people, activities, substances, to a bank balance, and even to a job. Our ego gets attached to anything it thinks will deliver the unconditional love for which it is constantly searching."

"Sounds like fly paper!"

"Now *there's* an image," Charmaine exclaimed. "One of the world's major sources of suffering is attachment to stubbornly 'stuck' and long-held beliefs. When I talk about forming attachment to outcome, I'm talking about our ego attaching its perceived happiness or well-being to some point in the future. That future may only be a few seconds ahead or years off."

"But it's enough to distract us from being fully present and free to be at our best here and now," William said, nodding thoughtfully.

"Yes, your ego tends to have its own patterns for forming these attachments. If you always *have* to watch a particular TV show, or sit on a *particular* bench at the park, or need a guarantee that your relationship or job will be the same tomorrow as it is today, you *will* live to some degree in anxiety and fear."

"And I'm not saying you should avoid a particularly nice bench at the park if you prefer it. I'm just suggesting that if you believe your happiness *depends* on it you won't be totally at ease."

"So pinning your *happiness* on it is the issue."

"Precisely," said Charmaine. "Having a preference for nice things is okay, but if you think your happiness depends on it - that's a horse of a different color. It is especially true if you begin to behave in ways that don't nurture your soul, in order to have those preferences."

"So," William repeated, "a preference that your ego thinks it must have in order to be happy is an attachment."

"Yes!"

"Now I understand the difference."

"Greed is another form of attachment," she continued. "We've seen personal and corporate greed ruin the happiness of many lives. Many people don't see greed as a negative force in their life. Some have even suggested that it's a good thing. But greed, like all attachments, is a soul-robbing activity in any form it takes. It's part of ego's very common notion that 'more is better'."

"Yet," William thought, "There must be a difference between greed and a healthy ambition to do well..."

"That difference manifests itself when we identify with our ego rather than our soul," Charmaine agreed.

"The phrase, 'soul-robbing activity' catches my attention every time you say it, Charmaine. I get the creepy feeling that the boogie man is about to reach out from under the bench and grab my ankle. What do you mean by 'soul-robbing'? It sounds pretty ominous."

"Good! Because it is," she said. "A soul-robbing activity is anything that pulls you away from your soul. If I have to give up part of who I am in order to have a job, a relationship, espouse a cause or even to enjoy a substance - food, drink or otherwise - then I can't afford that activity in my life. It becomes *toxic to me.* If I continue in that activity, it'll create symptoms in my body, my relationships, my work and especially in my ability to open my heart to myself and connect with my soul."

"I guess that about covers it," he said. "I have some thinking to do on that!"

Charmaine stopped to gaze at the hippos lounging in their expertly engineered jungle habitat.

"Most of us in this *corporate* jungle have become very goal-oriented. We also get emotionally attached to things, even other people, which we think we need for our own personal happiness. We look outside ourselves because we feel something is missing inside. We keep looking for something to fill the hole. 'Is this all there is?' we wonder. We end up tense and stressed."

"You're reciting the story of my life!"

"Of most peoples' lives," said Charmaine. "It's more of a spiritual crisis than a physical one. We keep trying to manipulate the outside world in order to get what we want. But if your happiness, your peace, your self-worth or your sense of security and well-being depend on having things a certain way, you're setting yourself up for a lot of pain and suffering."

"So how do I let go and let things be? I'm a practical sort of guy. I need some down-to-earth suggestions."

"This may sound oversimplified, but again, truth is simple. For starters, William, be generous, patient and appreciative."

"That sounds *too* simple."

"Give it a try and see. It may be *simple* but it's not necessarily *easy.*"

"I suppose," said William, "if everyone in our corporate world cultivated those three simple qualities, life would be just about perfect, wouldn't it?"

"Yes, because generosity of spirit teaches something about the inner ability to let go. And patience helps release attachments naturally. Appreciation focuses on love rather than fear.

"What do you mean, 'Patience helps release attachments *naturally?*"

"In order to be patient you must let go of the past, let go of being right, and in particular, let go of the attachment to what *might* happen," Charmaine explained. "Being free of an attachment is a byproduct of patience - a natural outcome."

"I'm all for 'natural', William said, reaching down to pick up a peanut bag and toss it into the trash.

"Letting go and releasing your attachments is the most calming and freeing thing you can do to detach yourself from your ego. Worrying about results and outcomes breeds fear and anxiety. Isn't that what you've been going through lately?"

"In spades!"

"It's hard to relax and enjoy life if you're always worrying about results and what other people think. How can you be open and spontaneous if you're trying to control every outcome?"

"It is a full-time job, that's for sure."

"Letting go of attachment to outcome frees you from stress and many of the physical symptoms that accompany stress."

"I get it! How can I let go of attachments all the time? *That* would be a full-time job, too!"

"You can't. So you might as well let go of that one, too," Charmaine said. "Remember, always trying to let go of every attachment *is* an attachment in itself. Do you recall how we talked about the ego and the soul and how the ego is always trying to gain control?"

"Yes."

"Trying to control the results is an ego-driven activity. All we can really do is attend to our *intention* and the *quality of energy* we put in. Situations and other people are one hundred per cent out of our control. It doesn't mean you shouldn't care about what happens and what others do. In fact, it may mean caring a great deal, but you can learn to let things be and suspend your expectations: to let go of the illusion of being in control, let go of trying to control the behaviors of others. You can grant others the freedom to find their own way."

"I can see that, in the quiet of this moment with you," said William. "But it's difficult to remain calm when stressful stuff is happening all around me, especially at work."

"Earlier we talked about living in moments of now and how being unattached to the results of your work frees you to be fully present with your work. Letting go of attachment *is being here, now*. Practice letting go of the past and stop worrying about the future. As best you can, *live in the moment*. It's a prescription for detachment, a prescription for happiness."

"But sometimes things just don't work out even when I have the best intentions and I've been fair and worked hard on something. What then?"

"Try developing a trust in the Universe, William. Have faith. From the perspective of the infinite safety and peacefulness of the soul you will realize the abundance of the world. And if it feels that life is not meeting your physical and emotional needs, allow your soul to guide you."

"But how?"

"You may not always know that, but if you have faith, you know you'll be okay. Detachment from a particular outcome is really another way of saying you have faith in the Universe. Attachment is based in fear - the fear that we will not get this thing or that outcome. Or that once we get it, we will lose it."

"Me, again," said William softly. "Right on the money!"

"Fear forces you to focus on the deficits in your life, doesn't it," asked Charmaine sympathetically. "The detached person focuses on the abundance in life."

"So I'd better start counting my blessings," he said. "I really do have so many, when I take the time to look for them."

"We all do," said Charmaine.

"It would make my life easier if others understood letting go of attachments better," William said wistfully.

"You can't worry about what others do. Remember, *the power of an open heart is that a closed heart can not stay closed in its presence.* Their heart will either open or they will go away until they are ready to open their heart. You *can*, however, practice letting go of trying to change others. You're only likely to see change in them when you change yourself. The most you can ever do to really help others is to open your own heart."

"That sounds harder."

"Here," she said stopping at a kiosk, "let me buy you a latté."

She handed him a steaming coffee as they walked on toward the amphibian display.

"You *can* learn to stop manipulating situations and other people in an attempt to get what you want."

"I thought that's how we're supposed to do it!"

Charmaine saw that William was just teasing, so she continued.

"As long as you're looking outside your deeper self, in the external world, for the Source of your needs, you'll feel vulnerable and insecure."

"Which needs?"

"All of them. That includes your sense of happiness, security and self-worth."

"The billions of advertising dollars spent to convince me of what I need, to be happy, doesn't make it easier. Credit card debt and bankruptcies indicate how keeping up with the Jones' has us all forming attachments, doesn't it?"

"It certainly can influence us," Charmaine agreed. "But a high-quality life has a lot more to do with what you *remove* from it rather than what you add. Usually the more obstacles and objects you remove from your life, the more satisfying life becomes."

William thought about the uncomfortable incidents that happened regularly at the office. He wondered what Charmaine would say about the stress he encountered on a fairly regular basis.

"My boss is so impatient. He always wants to get involved with details that aren't necessary for him to know. Now I've started to act that way, too."

"Many managers," she suggested, "border on being what some call 'control freaks'. It probably means they're feeling pressured and living with a high degree of stress and tension, too."

"Oh. I hadn't thought of that."

"So, it might not be useful to think it's all their fault. Supervisors often push because they too are responding similarly to pressure from above. But no matter the reason! Bosses must also find a balance between control and surrender, if they're to be successful. The more serious issue? When they react with impatience, they devalue themselves and their connection to the Divine."

"How is that?"

"Well, impatience is a failure to trust in the Source. It implies that we think we're separate from everyone and everything."

William and Charmaine came upon a bench tucked in a vine-green alcove overlooking the lion's domain. With unspoken agreement, they sat down and watched the cubs playing like kittens with their mother's twitching tail.

"You know," William said, breaking the comfortable silence, "the wisdom of the Clues has given my life a whole new direction. I'm already seeing small but significant changes in my life. Like, lately

I've spent more time feeling happy than depressed."

"I've noticed."

"And even with pressures at work I feel more confident in handling things. I'm starting to spend more time with other people. My home feels better to me, and other than being tired this week I've been feeling a little healthier."

"That's all such good news, William!"

"I start playing softball in a recreational league next weekend, which should be fun. Charmaine, you've helped me at a time when I really was in the pits."

"It's truly my pleasure. I've also learned from you, William."

"What could you possibly have learned from me?"

"You remind me just how special life is - how important it is to reach out and then let go. I may know these things at one level, but integrating them into my life is a lifelong process for me, too. We all need each other, you know, because we take turns being the student and the teacher."

"But you seem to have it all together."

"Ah, William," Charmaine said, smiling with tenderness, "have you ever noticed that people tend to work in the area of their own greatest need? You've been a help to me, too."

"Well, it's good to know I can help someone just by being me! Thanks for letting me know that."

"My pleasure, again," said Charmaine. She took a deep breath of the soft, fragrant air. Would you like me to show you the breathing technique for 'letting-go' that my grandfather taught me?"

"By all means."

"It's a simple but powerful way to reclaim your natural connection with your soul," Charmaine began. "Think of a 'letting-go' breath as a mini-meditation. It only takes four or five seconds."

"Perfect! I can do anything that takes only four or five seconds," William said with relief.

"First, it's important to know that your breath can be a passageway to your soul."

"You lost me."

"I visualize it as a stream of light going right to my core. Does that help?"

"Yeah, it really does."

"You can learn to use your breath with loving intention to enter into your open-heartedness."

"Not computing..."

"Just stay with me, William. You'll soon see the concept isn't as elusive as you think," Charmaine said reassuringly. "Let's just try it. When it feels right to you - and you'll know the moment - simply get present with yourself and take a breath. Nothing fancy, just take a normal breath.

"Okay."

"As you allow the air to fall out of your body, soften your eyes and your tongue and your belly.

"Charmaine?"

"Hmm?"

"I think I can get my mind around how to soften my tongue and belly, but how do I soften *my* eyes?"

"To soften your eyes, close them and then imagine gazing effortlessly, allowing them to be out of focus with nothing to see. To soften your tongue, imagine allowing it to become heavy and loose in your mouth. It's just lying there with nothing to say. There's a feeling of releasing any tension and simply letting go. Now in those four or five seconds, practice letting go of holding on to anything being of any importance at all. I'm not saying things are not important. Your ego would never stand for that. But I am suggesting you become masterful in your ability to let go of *holding on to their importance* for just a few moments. This isn't about letting go of things mattering *forever*. It's about becoming skillful at *completely letting go* of things mattering for just the few seconds it takes for the air to fall out of your body. This will help your ego practice surrendering the illusion of control."

"Okay, I can do that."

"Try it right now, then," said Charmaine. "Letting go is a skill. The more you practice, the better you get and the more you will see the results in your life."

William took a breath and as he began to release the air, he softened his eyes and his tongue and his belly. It took a few seconds for all the air to fall out of his body. He was quiet for a moment. The simple little exercise felt wonderfully freeing to him.

"Should I push the air out while I'm letting my breath fall out?"

"No. Just think of surrendering to your soul. Allow your breath to simply fall out of your body. This is not intended as a cleansing breath - just a moment of release, of letting go of the illusion of control over anything."

He drew another breath. He noticed it was easier to soften his eyes, his tongue and his belly this time.

"Just as I began to let the air out," said William, "I noticed it seemed to require a certain *willingness* to let go - like there's a decision to make - to let go or not to let go."

"That's your ego thinking about whether or not it's safe, even for a few seconds," said Charmaine quietly. "You may notice sometimes it just won't let go. If that happens just say to your ego, 'There, there, you don't have to let go right now if you don't want to.'"

"Really?"

"Really. This exercise isn't about setting up an adversarial relationship with the ego. The soul loves the ego with great tenderness, compassion and patience. Remember, its need to be in control is misguided but innocent. You'll notice that in a few minutes you can try again and be able to let go just fine."

"Charmaine, how often do you practice the softening breath?"

"Honestly, I probably do it a hundred times a day or more. It's a very simple centering tool. I assure you, if you would practice one breath like this first thing in the morning, last thing at night and once every fifteen minutes throughout the day, you'll see a difference in your life within 24 hours - a difference you'll like. You'll notice you begin to take things less seriously without losing your passion for life. You'll begin to notice that you take things less personally even if someone is right in your face. You'll notice your intuition and your creativity are more available to you. You'll notice that your libido is more engaged, that all your senses of sight, sound, smell and touch are sharper. You'll notice your sense of humor improving. You'll begin to notice that you are more willing to ask for what you want and to say no to things that don't feel right. You'll notice that you are listening better and asking better questions. Everything starts feeling better."

"In just one day?"

"I'm not kidding, William. The key is to do it without regard to how you're feeling. Do it when you're feeling great. Do it when you're feeling lousy. Do it when you don't even know how you feel. You can do it anytime, anywhere." Charmaine took a breath, softened and let go as she said, "You don't even have to stop talking. It's a very personal thing and you'll be amazed that the simplicity of it can make such a difference. It is at one end of the spectrum of meditation. Think of it as one *mini-meditation.*"

"You're right, Charmaine. It wasn't as elusive as I thought it would be. It's actually very do-able, even for me. I've heard you mention meditation a couple of times. Tell me more."

"Meditation is the final Clue. Think of this one breath as the beginning of learning the essence of meditation. It's a moment of surrender for the ego which can take you directly to where your soul's love, mercy, power and compassion lie."

He turned to look directly at her. "That's exactly where I want to go."

Summary

Clue #6: Let Go of Attachment to Outcome.

Forming attachments is the source of all suffering. When you learn to practice letting go of attachment, you will discover that the sense of peace and joy you seek out in the world actually comes from and through your deeper self. Attachments include our addictions to people, activities, substances and beliefs. Attachment to unchallenged patterns of thinking is an almost universal cause of great suffering.

- Attachment to any physical, emotional or material belief is the most universal cause of suffering. Attachments are a form of addiction.

- If your happiness, peace, self-worth, sense of security or well-being depend on possessing things or having things be a certain way, you are setting yourself up for pain and suffering.

- Letting go of attachment to outcome does not mean you don't care about what happens. Your happiness simply does not depend on the result.

- Being fully present helps in letting go of attachment, you naturally produce your best outcome.

- Trying to control the results is an ego-driven activity. Circumstances and people are one hundred percent out of your control.

- Let go of trying to change the people around you. You are only likely to see a change in others when you change what's going on inside yourself.

- Develop a trust in the Universe. Have faith! Detachment from a particular outcome is really another way of saying you have faith in the Universe.

- As long as you're looking outside yourself in the external world for the 'source' of your happiness or self-worth, you will feel vulnerable and insecure.

- All attachment is based in fear. It is the fear that you will not get this thing or that outcome and therefore you will not get the love you need and want.

- Clinging to attachment generates fear and worry, and a lack of authenticity and spontaneity. It feeds impatience, cravings, guilt and shame.

- A 'softening breath' practiced many times a day can be a very effective way to practice letting go of attachment to outcome.

At Work

- Your happiness at work lies not so much in the results of what you do, but rather in the process of your efforts and clear intention.

- Let go of the results and outcomes of your work because taking credit, getting depressed, feeling guilty or placing blame are all unhealthy attitudes.

- Letting go of attachment to results allows you to be fully present and more effective at work.

- Greed is a 'soul-robbing' activity.

The Benefits of Understanding Letting Go of Attachment

You will find access to your timing, your balance, your intuition, creativity, power and your full integrity. It will free you from stress. You will become more generous, appreciative and patient.

Exercises

#1: "Helium Filled Balloons"

This exercise is a simple way to practice letting go of our ego's fearful attachment (holding on) to things in our life that are important to us. Our ego would never be willing to agree that things don't matter. This is not about letting go of things mattering. It is about letting go of our ego's need to *hold on* to their mattering. This is also not about letting go of things mattering forever. It is about developing your ability and inclination to *totally let go for just a few moments.* Letting go happens in a moment that you chose to release your ego's grip on an outcome. It is a little magic trick, a soulful slight of hand, we can learn to play on our ego to help us get back to our soul's perspective. This exercise can free us to be more present and effective in everything we do.

Step 1: Find a quiet, warm place to lie down. Make yourself as comfortable as possible. Take a few softening breaths and close your eyes. See if you are willing to relax and let go of any concerns for the next 15 minutes.

Step 2: Now imagine you are holding in your hand numerous strings attached to helium filled balloons. One contains the future of your primary relationship. One is filled with what you are going to have for lunch tomorrow. Another is filled with what you are going to do this weekend. One is filled with what's happening in the Middle East. One contains the children starving in Africa. One contains problems you are having with your boss. One contains the hatred and bigotry we see in some places in our own society. And one contains what color socks you are going to wear tomorrow.

Step 3: Some of these balloons contain issues that seem just too big to let go of holding on to their mattering. So think about one of the balloons that does not feel so important such as what color socks you are going to wear tomorrow and see if you are willing to let go of holding on to your attachment to that mattering.

Step 4: If you are willing to let go, take a breath and imagine opening your hand as if releasing the string attached to that one helium-filled balloon. When you open your hand with the intention of letting go of that one string, you will discover that in that moment all the strings and all the balloons float away.

Principle

Some things seem too big to let go of. So think of something small and you will be able to let go. In a moment when you choose to "let go" you are *totally* letting go. When you open your hand you can't just let go of one string. By letting go you can free yourself from the fear-based place where attachment to outcome keeps you stuck, ineffective, imprisoned by your own clinging. No matter how righteous or noble your cause, you are more effective when you are free from attachment to the outcome of your actions.

Once you become comfortable with the idea and the experience of *letting go* you will find you can do it very quickly, anywhere, any time with any issue. You won't have to use the 'slight of hand' to free yourself from the fear based attachments that seem to continue to develop without our even noticing them. By practicing letting go of attachment to outcome, you can enter into your natural, deeper state of being fully present in the moment. It is in that space that your backbone and your open-heartedness reside. It is where you will find your wisdom, intuition, creativity, timing and balance to empower you in your commitment to make a real difference in the world in which we all live.

#2. "Letting Go of Attachment to Limited Thinking"

This exercise is about freeing ourselves from mediocre, autopilot patterns of unconscious and limited thinking. It is designed to help you clarify your desire and your ability to have passionate, energizing jobs and relationships. It is about embracing commitment.

Most of us desperately want commitment in our lives but we are terrified of the idea. There are two reasons for this.

One. We are afraid that if we were to *totally* commit to our relationship or job that we would have to give up some part of who we are.

> *False.* It is true that commitment requires compromise and give and take. But it does not require you to give up any part of who you are at the core of your being.

Two. We are afraid that if we *totally* commit it means *forever* and we just can't get our heads around forever. It's too big.

> *False.* Commitment is not about forever. It is about 100 percent right now, today. This exercise does not mean to imply that we are not interested in being in our relationships forever.

In fact, this exercise is precisely about how we can increase the likelihood of being in a committed relationship for our entire life. The *experience* of commitment can only occur in a *moment of now*. It is our ongoing commitment to being present in the moment that will take us to life long relationships. It is only our fear of the *idea* of forever that keeps us from being fully present and totally committed in the moment. This exercise will help us get past that fear.

Step 1: Prepare for this exercise by allowing yourself an extra 10 to 15 minutes undisturbed in bed tomorrow morning before you have to get up.

Step 2: As you awake in the morning ask yourself a big, life changing question, such as:
    "Am I going to quit my job today?"
    "Am I going to disown my teenager today?"
    "Am I going to leave my relationship today?"
    Look deep inside and tell the truth. In most cases the answer is going to be no. The question is simply a wake-up call to invite you to live life at a higher level of integrity.

Step 3: If the answer is *no,* then ask yourself if you are willing to be in that relationship/job *today* with a *100 per cent commitment* to bring all you have to make it the best it can be, to do whatever it takes to be the best boss, the best worker, the best partner, the best parent you can possibly be. Make the commitment for today. Don't let the thought of *forever* scare you out of *going for it* today.
    If the answer is *yes,* then get up and do it. If you really do feel you have to give up a part of who you are in order to be in that relationship or job than you can *not* afford to have that job or relationship in your life. It becomes a soul-robbing influence. Start thinking about what it would take for you to leave. Talk to trusted friends. Get input and start thoughtfully planning an exit strategy. Whatever you do, do it with respect and compassion; be clear, be strong and be fully present each step of the way.

Step 4: Ask yourself, "What would it look like if I gave this relationship/job absolutely everything I could and to do so in a way that would truly nurture my soul *today?*"

Step 5: Make a list of habits that reflect higher levels of commitment. Here is a sample list:

• Tell the truth. Tell the truth. Tell the truth.

• Show up. Be emotionally and physically present and available.

• Listen in such a way that others actually feel heard.

• Be on time.

- Keep every agreement you make.

- Make no agreements you do not fully intend to keep.

- Set appropriate boundaries. Learn how to say no if something doesn't feel right.

- Learn to give generously without withholding and also without its becoming a soul robbing activity.

- Ask for what you want. This is not selfish. To ask for what you want is to have integrity, to tell the truth about who you are and what you really need and want.

- Apologize. Make amends. Make things as right as you can.

- Practice defenselessness.

- Tell on yourself.

- Take exquisite care of yourself. Pay attention to diet, exercise, sleep and addictive substances (drugs, alcohol, nicotine, caffeine).

- Be gentle with yourself and be in balance in all things.

Step 6: Wake up tomorrow and ask yourself the same questions. If the answer is no, then see if you are willing to get totally into whatever it is. If the answer is yes, then do it.

Principle

Letting go of attachment to limited thinking requires being totally present *in the moment*.

To be totally present in the moment means to be totally *committed*.

To be totally committed is to be free of attachment to the *idea* of *forever.*

Commitment is not about forever. It is about 100 per cent right now, which is all we ever have to work with. Ironically, this commitment to be totally present in the moment is what will ultimately lead us to the lifelong, committed relationships we desire.

To totally commit does not mean having to give up some part of who you are. It is about bringing all of who you really are to your relationship, job or cause.

Chapter Nine

Clue # 7

Forgiveness: A Gift that Transforms the Giver

The more William learned from the ancient wisdom in the Clues, the more he wanted to learn. But a couple of things kept bothering him. Remembering what he'd learned about honesty and suffering, William decided to tell the truth - to tell on himself. It was time to go toward some of his old hurt feelings and deal directly with his pain. The thought was a little scary, but he knew Charmaine would help him out.

William was walking back from the waterfall where he'd come to enjoy relaxing in the warm sun beside the pool. He loved the light mist spraying over him from the towering waterfall above. Charmaine called it a 'soulful water massage'. William chuckled, remembering how they'd laughed and sung there only a few weeks before. He had learned so many important things since then. He felt happier than he could remember being in years. But right now he needed more input.

As he rounded a bend in the path, Charmaine was sitting under a maple tree, tossing popcorn to a local squirrel.

"Hey," she said, patting the grass next to her. "I was just thinking about you."

"You have an uncanny ability for sensing when I need to talk," William exclaimed, sitting beside her. "I'm so glad you're here," he said. "I've been doing great lately but..."

"But...?" Charmaine waited.

"Well, I've been missing my family quite a bit. I know I need to contact them, but I'm struggling with how my father was so unavailable to me."

"A problem with your dad."

"Yes, and you know, I'm still mad at him for not being there when I needed him! Some days I blame my father for all my unhappiness. And it's weird, but I have similar feelings when I think about my boss. He continually shows no interest in how I feel or how hard I work. The more I think about it, the madder I get! I just can't forgive either of them for how badly they treated me."

"Forgiveness is not about them," Charmaine answered. "It's about you."

William grinned good-naturally. "Why doesn't that surprise me?"

"Understanding that forgiveness is *a gift that transforms the giver* is the next Clue."

"Good - perfect timing! It's time to deal with my anger toward my father, because it has a way of creeping into my everyday life. So, let's hear it," William said with an earnestness that made Charmaine smile.

"Though forgiveness is the soul's natural state of being, forgiving isn't easy."

"Swell," said William, drooping a little.

"For the ego, that is, forgiveness is very difficult," she said. "It's so difficult because the ego thinks if it totally forgave somebody, it would have to give up part of who it is. It would have to give up its stories of the past, and let go of its evidence against the offender - all those righteous and apparently legitimate bad feelings that keep old wounds open and raw. To forgive, our ego would have to be willing to feel vulnerable and powerless, to let go of being in control."

"That sounds a lot like *my* ego, all right," William nodded.

"That sounds like *all* our egos," Charmaine said. "It would rather be right, cling to its evidence and justifiably hurt feelings than get what it wanted in the first place."

"What did it want in the first place?"

"To be happy, be at peace - and be loved! But the anticipation of forgiving is like facing the firing squad, to our ego. Once again, the ego is innocent in its intention but totally mistaken in its conclusion."

"Man, I can really see that in myself," said William. "I can't resist talking about what a jerk my boss is, instead of understanding the pressure he's under, and forgiving him. But it's hard to forgive him when I know he'll do the same thing tomorrow. The same is true with my father. If I forgave him for ignoring me, and we reconnected, he might do the same thing again. I'd feel like a fool."

"And you're right to be skeptical about anything changing," said Charmaine. "In fact, it's quite likely to happen again."

"So what's the point?"

"Your ego thinks forgiveness means being weak, vulnerable and foolish. And sometimes our ego likes being a victim. It makes it easier to not forgive. It's also hard to forgive if you can't be certain the same thing won't happen again."

"That's true!"

"Forgiving generally requires what is natural for our soul and difficult for our ego. It requires healthy boundaries and the clarity to take care of yourself, to make certain the same thing won't happen again. You may have to let go of wanting something from the other person that they simply don't have to give or that they refuse to give. You'll find forgiveness much easier if you feel safe."

"So what are healthy boundaries?" William asked with interest.

"A willingness to say no to things that don't feel right, that drain your energy."

"But I always feel someone will be upset with me if I say *no*."

"Many of us have a very low tolerance for conflict and disharmony," said Charmaine. "So we go along with what really doesn't feel right for us, actually giving away our own personal power. Having healthy boundaries sometimes requires a willingness to allow certain people be unhappy or disappointed. We can't give up who we are to please everyone around us."

"Well, that makes sense, since you can never please everyone anyway," William added.

"Let's go up to the bridge," Charmaine suggested, rising and brushing a couple of leaves off her skirt. "It's such a soul-nurturing place. Places like that make it easier to do inner work."

"It does feel like a pretty powerful place," said William. "I've experienced some intense feelings there. Not to mention some really beautiful moments. Is it possible that a place can have its own energy?"

"It is indeed," she answered, and they started up the trail toward the bridge. "There are some places that just seem to nurture your soul - make you feel strong, peaceful and safe - like the bridge and the waterfall. Other places can feel just the opposite. Pay attention to those feelings. They can be a useful guide."

"Now, about your father. When you were a child the problem was that you didn't get the love and timely support you richly deserved and needed from him."

"That's right, I didn't!"

"It's quite likely that given who he is at the core of his being and what his life was like at the time, he simply didn't have it to give."

"Hmm! That never occurred to me..."

"But now, you continue to want those things from him knowing he may not have them to give."

"I see the problem."

"It's a problem only you can solve," said Charmaine. "This is where understanding the *gift of suffering and letting go of attachments* is particularly helpful."

Unsure where Charmaine was headed, William waited expectantly for her to continue.

"Consider grieving for what was not there, then letting go of continuing to want it. If you can do that, you'll find it much easier to forgive your dad and free yourself from your bad feelings."

"But I still want that feeling of being loved and supported," William lamented.

"Of course you do. We all do. But the world was never wired up to give us all the love and support we need, not in the size package or at the time or in the way we want it. That's why the fourth Clue, *Loving Yourself* is so important. Your soul is your access point to infinite love. When you learn to open your heart to yourself, you have access to exactly what your ego is looking for in the only place it knows to look - out in the world. Only when your ego lets go of demanding that it get what it wants from the world of physical reality, can it finally surrender and open to your soul's infinite supply of love and support. Then you begin to bring that quality of love and support *to* your world rather than continue to desperately seek it out *in* your world."

"So," William said, setting up a scenario, "a guy gets home from a good day at work, in a great mood, and he smiles and kisses his wife only to have her turn away and say - 'Leave me alone!' Are you saying he can learn not to get upset or take it personally, because maybe she had a hard day and her reaction has nothing to do with him?"

"Yes, that's right," said Charmaine. "When he comes home with an open heart, he brings his love *to* his wife. He can tell her he loves her, tell her he's available if she wants to talk about her feelings and give her some space. He can remind himself that all of us deserve the right to feel moody sometimes. He can learn to detach for the moment and care for himself while she has the time to process her feelings."

"And here's the irony," Charmaine continued, "the more we let go of that ego-driven neediness, the more likely we are to actually receive love and support in our own world. But then that love and support is a *bonus.* The basic love we all need is always accessed from within. By finding our source of love within, we are also more able to give love and support to others when they need it. Forgiveness is one way to open that doorway to the soul, William."

"It's so amazing that letting go of needing something makes it more likely to come my way."

"Isn't it? And it just happens to be true."

"You know, Charmaine, I have trouble with the idea of having to forgive *forever.* The idea of committing to anything forever totally freaks me out."

"The notion of forever is a real deal-breaker to the ego," Charmaine said with a laugh. "But forgiveness is not about forever. It's about letting go completely, one hundred percent, *right now.*"

"Ah," William said, remembering his lessons with a grin, "because all we really ever have are moments of now."

"Exactly. Forgiveness can only happen in a moment of now. It has nothing to do with forever. Forgiveness is also not something that you can hold onto. You may find it necessary to forgive several times to get completely free of the pain of *unforgiveness.* Forgiveness is saying, 'In this moment of now I totally and completely forgive.' In that single moment of awareness, there is neither past nor future - only now. And if we forgive, we experience peace."

"I see how these Clues all fit together," William said. "Seeing suffering as a gift and learning to go toward it to learn what there is to learn; living in the moment; choosing soul over ego; loving and being honest with yourself; letting go of attachment to outcome and discovering that forgiveness is a gift that transforms the giver are all doorways to the soul. This is pretty powerful stuff! Can I ever hope to realize all these benefits?"

"You've already experienced many moments of now in which you've benefited from these principles, William. I've been practicing for a long time and I can't do it all the time. But it's okay. The concepts contained in the Clues just work and the more I practice them the more I see results in my life. Living the Clues is more a journey than a destination, and this is just the beginning!"

"I sure feel hopeful," William exclaimed. "Even though forgiving is not my strong suit...."

"One of the secrets to forgiveness is accepting the difficulty of forgiving. Acceptance leads to change. Feelings like resentment, anger, fear, guilt, blame, vindictiveness and spite originate in your thoughts. The hurt you feel comes from your own thoughts, not from what some other person did or did not do to you."

"I get it! You mean I have no one to blame for my hurt feelings?"

"No," said Charmaine, chuckling at William's display of mock horror. "And whoever has offended you doesn't have to be involved, or present or even alive, for you to forgive them. And they certainly don't need to apologize to you as a prerequisite to you forgiving them! That may be one more thing you'll need to let go of. Forgiveness has everything to do with you, not the one who has offended you. Forgiveness is a powerful healer and has a great transformative value."

"I have a feeling you're about to tell me *how* great," William said affectionately.

"The great value of forgiveness is freedom - freedom from all those bad feelings you harbor against others. So, you'll have more peace in your life and more energy. You'll find it easier to feel compassion and empathy for all, not just those who've offended you. You'll be healthier. *Un*forgiveness, like spite and revenge, is a poison that affects not only your thinking but your body. Remember, the mind and body are one organism. Nothing affects one without the other being affected. Physical health, particularly in cardiovascular terms, is better in those who forgive than those who do not. Cancers, ulcers, fatigue, tension headaches and stomach irritations may also be aggravated by an unwillingness to forgive. Similarly, your emotional health is adversely affected by anger, long-held resentments and bitterness. Unforgiveness is not a benign emotional activity. It's another 'soul-robbing' activity. It has its price."

"Which is always too high," said William. "I can see the value of forgiveness, but how do I do it? What are the mechanics of forgiveness?"

"Let's just sit for a few moments and take in the scene. They watched the hustle and bustle of the city far below, practicing a few softening breaths.

After a bit Charmaine spoke.

"All forgiveness, you know, starts with self-forgiveness. You'll find it much easier to forgive someone if you have first forgiven yourself. For example, is there something in regard to your father for which you have not yet forgiven yourself?"

William remained silent for a long time.

"Well, actually there are a couple of things," he said finally. "One time I was so angry at him I didn't give him anything for Father's Day. I totally ignored him. Sometimes I behaved pretty defiantly, like the time I lied to him about using his new car. I've felt badly about those things but I was just so mad at him for working all the time and ignoring me! He never went to even one of my baseball games. It's hard to let that old stuff go."

"For now, let's separate your feelings toward your boss from the hurt and anger you feel about your father," Charmaine suggested. "One reason you're struggling so much with forgiving your boss is because it really doesn't have much to do with your boss. Think of it this way, William. *Every man is your father until you have emancipated yourself from him.* The same can be said that every *woman is your mother until you have emancipated yourself from her.* I realize this is a generalization..."

"Wait a minute! What do you mean, 'emancipate' myself from my father?'"

"When you only see him in his role as your *father*, you have certain expectations that he didn't meet. When you let go of holding on to your old view of him, you can begin to see him as a *man* with room for faults and shortcomings, like all of us. You can then begin to let go of wanting things from him that he wasn't able to give you when you were young. Keep in mind that he *still* may not have them to give. As an adult, you can begin to accept and appreciate who he is rather than struggle with who he is *not*."

"That could change everything," said William. "I don't think I know who my father really is. I never gave him a chance."

"Be gentle with yourself. It's understandable; we all go through those struggles. When you start exploring your feelings, you may be amazed how often they are the very same ones you felt toward your parents when you were young. We attach a lot of our current anger to old hurts, without even realizing it. When you want to forgive, it may help to first see if there is anything for which you have not yet forgiven your parents. If you are willing to do that, you'll be amazed how much easier it is to forgive others. It's also helpful to focus on one person at a time. Our ego will use any excuse to stay a little fuzzy and unclear. Another case of 'fuzziphelia'."

"Fuzziphelia," William laughed. "I've definitely had a serious case of that! But I'm getting past it. I *want* to get clear about my thoughts and feelings. So, I'm ready to give forgiveness a try."

"Let's start with the biggie then."

"Yeah, let's start with the biggie," William agreed wholeheartedly. "What's the biggie?"

"You," she smiled. "Then we'll take on the other biggie."

"Let me guess," he grinned. "My father."

The Mechanics of Forgiveness

"The mechanics of forgiveness start by taking a 'letting-go' breath. Just take a breath, soften as best you can and for the moment, let go of holding on to anything being of any importance at all as you allow the air to fall out of your body. This is one way your ego allows your soul's love, mercy and compassion to come in."

William took a slow, deep breath, then let himself soften, from the inside out.

"Now look to see if you feel *willing* to forgive yourself for the hurtful things you felt you did to your father.

"Okay, I'm as willing as I know how to be," he said tentatively.

"Willingness is a key to being able to forgive. If you don't feel ready, wait a few moments, draw another letting-go breath and take a fresh look."

William paused a moment, then took another breath.

"I'm having a little trouble letting go," he admitted.

"It takes some practice," Charmaine reassured him. "To find access to the Divine within you, you must first accept yourself exactly as you are. All your faults and imperfections are part of being an everyday human being. True self-acceptance is saying, 'My heart is open to me.' *Complete self-acceptance eliminates the need for self-forgiveness.* So remember, accepting yourself and your true feelings is the first step to moving through them."

"It feels a little like moving through thick mud," William chuckled.

"Sometimes it helps to look at your reflection in a mirror. Look straight at yourself and say, 'I totally forgive you for the hurtful behavior toward your father. I love you and I forgive you.' Sometimes it helps to close your eyes and simply imagine seeing yourself at the age you were at the time of the act and repeat those words."

William felt surprised by the directness of the statement. He took another breath, softened, closed his eyes and said, "I totally forgive you for your hurtful behavior toward your father. I love you and I forgive you."

"Take another breath and say it again," she suggested.

And William did.

"Remember, this is your soul talking to your ego. It can be very healing. Say it every half hour or so and see if you begin to feel lighter about those things you did to your father. You might even begin to feel a little lighter about some of the things your father did to you. Given who you were at the time, and what you needed and felt you weren't getting, you might see that what you did makes perfect sense. Remember, the source of all our hurtful or destructive behavior simply comes out of a *reaction* to not getting the love our ego thinks it needs and wants."

"Now I think I understand why you use the phrase 'innocent but misguided'. It really does come from an innocent motive."

"Forgiveness requires a willingness to accept everyone's inherent innocence, including your own."

"Funny," he thought. "I usually feel far from innocent."

"You need to be willing to see the innocence of your own hurt and frustration. Of course it doesn't justify inappropriate behavior. It does help to regard yourself with tenderness and compassion. Sometimes we just aren't quite ready to let go of every hurt feeling. If that's the case, there is a little exercise you can do to check exactly where you are in regard to forgiving yourself or someone else."

"What's that? I can use all the help I can get," said William.

"It often helps to have someone to do this with. So I want you to look me square in the eye, maintain eye contact with me and repeat exactly what I say. I want you to say it as though you were telling me the absolute truth. Each time I say something repeat it, take a breath and then look inward to see if it feels true."

"Okay, but this feels more than a little weird. I sure hope nobody is watching."

Charmaine looked William in the eye with no expression at all and began the exercise.

Forgiveness Exercise

*"I **totally** forgive myself for my hurtful and unkind acts toward my father."*

William quickly looked away. He brought his eyes back to Charmaine and said, "I totally forgive myself for my hurtful and unkind acts toward my father." He then took a breath and tried to notice how he felt.

Charmaine maintained expressionless eye contact. She waited a few moments and said, *"I'm **not yet ready** to totally forgive myself for my hurtful and unkind acts toward my father."*

Again William's eyes shifted away but quickly returned his attention to Charmaine.

"I'm *not yet ready to totally* forgive myself for my hurtful and unkind acts toward my father." William took another breath and noticed his feelings.

Charmaine said, *"I **do not** forgive myself for my hurtful and unkind acts toward my father."*

William said, "I *do not* forgive myself for my hurtful and unkind acts toward my father." He steadfastly maintained eye contact and took another breath.

Charmaine said, *"I **will not** forgive myself for my hurtful and unkind acts toward my father **no matter what it costs me.**"*

William looked away, then came back to Charmaine's eyes.

"I *will not* forgive myself for my hurtful and unkind acts toward my father *no matter what it costs me.*"

"So which of those feels the most accurate?" asked Charmaine.

"That last one was really hard to say," said William. "But I think the second one, 'not yet being ready to *totally* forgive', was the closest to where I am right now. I'd like the first one to be true but it just isn't."

"It's okay. At first, most of us find the second one feels more true. But I've seen some people whose egos are so poisoned, so stuck in a reactive place that the last one, 'not being willing to forgive no matter what it costs' is the truth for them. And if it is, then the first thing to do is open your heart to your own closed-heartedness. Remember: completely accepting yourself exactly where you are is the first step to moving through a difficult issue."

"That exercise was tough to do!"

"You did great. This isn't easy. Now look and see if there's some way you can take care of yourself so you don't repeat the behavior you can't forgive yourself for. For example, can you commit to never do those kind of things to your father again - no matter what?"

"Yes, I can. I would never do those things again, no matter what!"

"Good. Then look and see if there is something you need to do in order to fully forgive yourself, something you have not done yet."

The Apology

"Do you mean apologize to my father for my hurtful behavior? That would feel like eating crow in front of the one who hurt me the most. Is that really necessary?"

"Remember. Forgiveness has nothing to do with the other person. *Apologizing is also a gift that transforms the giver* if you do it right. The question is how badly do you want to get free of the bitter feelings you've been living with all these
years? Another benefit of forgiveness is that it keeps you in the present by letting go of the past. "

"Do I have to apologize to his face?"

"It would be most powerful that way but, no it's not necessary. Sometimes the person is dead and gone and it's impossible to clear the air in person. But you can do it right here, right now if you want."

"So how do I apologize?"

"There are four key elements to an apology that help free you from your bad feelings. The first element is to be openhearted and sincere. No patronizing or just mouthing the words here."

"The second key element is to acknowledge that *no matter what the other person ever did or did not do, they did not deserve to be treated the way you treated them.*"

"Oh, man," said William uncomfortably, "that's a hard one to swallow!"

"If someone treats you with disrespect William, it's no justification for you to treat them with disrespect. You treat them with respect simply because that's what you do if you want your life to work. It has nothing to do with the other person. It's just one of the ways the universe is set up."

"I can see that, but I sure know a lot of people who wouldn't agree with that notion."

"I know you're right, Charmaine said, "but how healthy are their lives and relationships? "

"I see your point."

"Now the third element of an apology is to apologize. Be specific about what you did and what you're sorry about. Acknowledge their feelings of hurt or pain. It's important to say, *'I'm sorry'* and mean it."

"Simple, but not easy," William said.

"The fourth element ," Charmaine continued, "is to *make a commitment to them – a commitment that you will do everything in your power to never treat them that way again.*"

"But..."

"And in a true apology William, you don't justify or explain your behavior. You never even mention the thing they did to you."

"Not even if..."

"You do not ask for anything in return, including their forgiveness. It is completely irrelevant to an honest apology."

William looked stunned. They sat silently for a time while he absorbed what Charmaine had said.

"So, are you ready to give it a try?"

"You mean right here, right now?"

"Yes. Just look out over the city in the direction of your home. Apologize to your father as though he were here. This may feel a little artificial and awkward, but it does work. Go ahead, try it."

"Well, okay, here goes." William closed his eyes and sat quietly for a few moments. He used his breath, as he had learned, to get to his willingness.

"Dad," he said, "I'm sorry. I really am! No matter what you ever did or did not do, you did not deserve to be treated the way I treated you. I ignored you on Father's Day, I lied to you about your car and I was often intentionally defiant. I know it must have hurt your feelings. It may have caused you to feel sad, angry and disappointed. I promise you I will do my best to never do anything like that again."

William sat quietly for a few minutes. A tear surfaced at the corner of his eye.

"That felt pretty good," he said with a loud, cleansing sigh. "And you know what? I do feel a little lighter."

He remembered a few other things he'd done. So he looked to the horizon again and added them to his apology.

"What a load off my chest," he exclaimed.

"Good. You know, apologizing and forgiving happen in a very intimate moment between your soul and ego."

"Really!"

"It's a moment of willingness to let go of all of the ego's defenses. When you surrender and go to the place where you are totally defenseless, you will find that it's also the place where you are infinitely safe. It's only the ego that ever needs defending or protecting. The soul is always completely safe and at peace."

"So tell me again in a nutshell, how do I surrender and get to that place where I'm defenseless but safe?"

"Breathe, soften and let go."

"Let go of what?"

"Let go of being right. Let go of all of your evidence and stories. Let go of your need to be special. Let go of the past. Let go of the future. Let go of the illusion of being in control. For that moment, let go of holding on to *absolutely anything* being of any importance at all. Surrender to your soul."

"I feel as if I've spent my whole life holding on to this stuff. It's funny ... "

"What's that?"

"Well, even though it feels scary, I think it'll be a huge relief when I can really begin to let go of all that stuff."

"I think you will be amazed at the difference it makes, William. By the way, your father is very lucky to have a son like you. Maybe someday he will appreciate that."

"Do you think?"

"If not, it will be a loss for both of you, but mostly for him. It really is amazing how you are moving ahead using the Clues. How do you feel right now?"

"I feel good, a little weird, a little energized and a little tired - but mostly I feel light. I just realized something! I still love my father, and I miss him. Come to think of it, I miss my mother and sister, too." Another tear slid down his cheek.

William and Charmaine sat quietly for a while.

"That was really helpful," said William. "Right now, I feel much better about my father. But let me make sure I've got this straight. If I'm having trouble forgiving someone, I first look to see if there is something I haven't forgiven myself for in regard to this person. Then I use my breath and my willingness to soften as a key to forgiving. I also need to make certain I've done what I need to do to take care of myself so the same thing won't happen again. For example, I need to make certain that I don't allow the person that hurt me to be in a position where they could ever do it again."

"I recognize and acknowledge their feelings. Oh, and I need to look and see if the problem could be that I'm still holding on to wanting something from them that they don't actually have to give me."

William furrowed his brow in thought.

"Could that be something as reasonable as wanting them to be nice to me, or fair, or just not to be mean to me?"

"It certainly could. Wanting others to treat you well at any given moment matters little if they don't have it to give. Neither your happiness nor your treatment of others should ever depend on how they treat you. Accept that, and it will be much easier to forgive."

"I can also use the four elements to an apology to check exactly where I am in the process of forgiving."

"Yes, in forgiveness and any other place you might get stuck, it's helpful to accept where you are. If you have a bad feeling, just breathe, soften and let it go. If it doesn't go, then accept it as the way you feel right then and give yourself permission to feel it. I call it opening your heart to your own closed-heartedness."

"This stuff isn't easy."

"No, it isn't, but these exercises are actually skills. The more you practice, the easier it gets and the more you'll see the results.

Forgiveness is a skill worth cultivating. It will help to remember that who others are at the core of their being and how they treat you may be two different things. Separate the person from the deed. There is *no one* who is not worthy of your compassion. They are responsible for what they do and you are responsible for your feelings about that behavior. If you knee-jerk react to them instead of behaving in a way that's consistent with your higher self, you give them power to determine how you feel and how you may behave."

"I'd be giving my power away!"

"If you seek a deeper understanding of why they did what they did, you'll often see an innocence beneath their reactive or unkind behavior."

"Won't they think I'm weak if I don't stick up for myself?"

"Having empathy and compassion needn't diminish your strength or the need to take care of yourself. If you feel really stuck in bad feelings, the source of the hurt is usually much older and deeper. They probably just *triggered* feelings that were already deeply rooted in you."

"So, what do I do about it?"

"Separate your feelings from what your 'little-mind' thinks caused them. It's a short-cut to deeper healing. Focus on what you're feeling rather than why your ego thinks you're feeling it."

"How?"

"Sometimes it helps to write a highly-charged letter. No editing or censoring is necessary or helpful. The purpose of the letter is in the *writing* of it. It's an unedited, direct way to express and get the feelings out of your system, to clear your mind. This letter is not intended to be sent, though you may later decide to send an edited version as part of your forgiveness process."

"It seems to me that the other guy gets all the breaks. What about being fair to *me?*"

"It's difficult for most of us to forgive because it seems unjust to ourselves. One of the biggest barriers to forgiveness is that it feels like the other person will get more out of it than we do. To our ego, forgiveness seems to undermine the urge to catch and punish the offender, defusing the righteous anger. Forgiving often feels like you're showing love to the one that did you harm, and thus showing a lack of love toward yourself, the harmed one."

"My thought, exactly."

"Or it may feel like if you forgive, you're condoning what they did or that it really wasn't that offensive."

"Right."

"That forgiving disarms revenge and revenge feels right and natural, like scratching an itch. We think it's our job to punish them. Our ego thinks that not forgiving protects us from being hurt again. It's like saying, 'If I stay angry, he'll stay on his best behavior.'"

"You know, Charmaine, sometimes it's really hard to remember that the things that happen in my life don't actually cause my feelings, but just *trigger* them. I can see how disempowering it is to stay in a 'blame' frame of mind, holding tenaciously to all my evidence against those who've wronged me."

"For many of us, it's really hard to let go of the grim satisfaction of revenge. Spite, vindictiveness, and retribution are poison to our lives. It's especially difficult when they're fed to us in movies, games and books. Revenge and pay-back are actually celebrated in our world. We see it at work in the oldest and most painful conflicts around the world. Global leaders use it to justify terrible acts of retribution that is then returned in-kind."

"It's a vicious circle," William agreed. "Do you think the people in the corporate world will ever learn the value of forgiveness?"

"Yes I do, William. When a sufficient number of us have suffered enough to no longer allow it to take a place, it will stop. Sometimes the tincture of time can heal old wounds. But if we keep scraping away the scab and re-injuring each other, it's difficult to heal. You see how ego tends to justify not forgiving?"

"I guess I do. That's how I've looked at things in the past. But that kind of thinking really doesn't help, does it?

Charmaine gently touched William's arm to emphasize the point she was about to make.

"We forgive those who have wronged us, not so much because they deserve to be forgiven, but because we love ourselves so much we refuse to keep paying again and again for the injustice. Forgiveness neutralizes bitterness. Remember: you can't hurt those who offend you by not forgiving them. You only hurt yourself."

"How would I keep paying for the injustice?"

"The price you pay are all the painful feelings that come from *un*forgiveness such as guilt, resentment, spite, vindictiveness, anger, depression, anxiety and *many* others," she answered.

"Forgiveness moves us from ego to soul. It's about letting go of the ego's tendency to cling to and cultivate the belief that we've been wronged. Forgiveness is letting go of the need to be right. Forgiveness is not about *condoning* hurtful behavior, *deciding to forget* offenses or even *reconciling* with the offender. Rather, it means giving up the ego's commitment to be aggravated, giving up the desire to strike back."

"It's hard to love those that hurt me so deeply."

"You don't have to love or even like those who hurt you," said Charmaine. "But you do have to respect their right to exist, to be different, to live their lives as they see fit, even those that have seriously wronged you."

"Definitely the high road," said William taking a steadying breath. "I can see why it's one not more traveled. There *is* a certain satisfaction in righteous indignation..."

"You nailed it right on the head," said Charmaine. "Many people are so wrapped up in their own perspectives and negative feelings, they don't stop to consider the feelings of others. But by forgiving them, you can release your own negative feelings and get on with your life. Even if you don't particularly like them, you can still forgive them, because that's what works best - and *you* will feel better."

"So forgiveness is actually more about not letting others determine my emotions or behavior."

"Right."

"Forgiveness is a way to reclaim ownership of the quality of my own life. If I forgive others, I set myself - not them - free. That is because *they* are the only ones that have the power to set themselves free. I can't do that for them. And if I try, it's just one more distraction from the only work I *can* do, which is to clean up my own life. I am the only one that can free myself from my own suffering!"

"Congratulations, William!" Charmaine laughed with delight.

"What for?"

"You've just passed this lesson on forgiveness, with flying colors."

Summary

Clue # 7
Forgiveness: A Gift that Transforms the Giver

Develop both your inclination and your ability to forgive yourself and others. Unforgiveness is a form of attachment that can cause great suffering. Like spite and revenge, it is a poison that will affect not only your thinking but your body. Learning to forgive can free you from guilt and resentment.

- Forgiving is a natural state of being of our soul.

- Forgiveness is not about the other person. It is all about you. Forgive those who wrong you, not so much for their benefit but because you are the only one who can forgive. You deserve the freedom from paying the high price of unforgiveness - anger, spite, revenge, vindictiveness and resentment.

- Forgiveness is difficult for our ego because it thinks that if it were to totally forgive it would have to give up some part of who it is. Even the anticipation of forgiving is like facing death to our ego.

- Another reason forgiveness is so difficult for our ego is because it thinks forgiveness means being weak, vulnerable and even foolish. It thinks the other person will get more out of it than we do.

- Forgiving is difficult because it seems unfair to our ego, which can sometimes enjoy being the victim. By not forgiving, the ego mistakenly thinks it is protecting itself from being hurt again.

- In order to fully forgive someone, you may have to let go of wanting something from them that they simply don't have to give or that they refuse to give you.

- All forgiveness starts with self-forgiveness. You'll find it much easier to forgive someone if you have first forgiven yourself for any wrong you may have done to him.

- Forgiveness requires healthy boundaries and the clarity to take care of yourself, to make certain the same thing will not happen again.

- Complete self-acceptance eliminates the need for self-forgiveness.

- Forgiveness can only happen in a moment of now. It has nothing to do with forever. It's about letting go completely, one hundred percent, right now.

- Forgiveness is not something that you can hold on to. It may be necessary to forgive several times to really get free of the pain of unforgiveness.

- Unforgiveness, like spite and revenge, is a poison that can effect your body as well as your attitude.

- Separate the person from the act. Forgiveness is about the person. Holding on to what they did to you simply gets in the way of forgiving.

- Forgiveness requires a willingness to accept everyone's inherent innocence, including your own.

The Apology

- *First:* Be openhearted and sincere.

- *Second:* Acknowledge that no matter what the other person did or did not do, they do not deserve to be treated in the way you treated them.

- *Third:* Apologize. Be specific about what you did and what you're sorry about. Acknowledge their feelings of hurt or pain. It's important to say, *'I'm sorry'* and mean it.

- *Fourth:* Make a commitment to that person – a commitment that you will do everything in your power to never treat her that way again.

At Work

- You don't have to love or even like everyone with whom you work. You do have to respect their right to exist, to be different and to live their own lives as they see fit.

The Benefits Of Understanding Forgiveness

Physical health, particularly in cardiovascular terms, tends to be better in those who forgive than in those who do not. Another benefit of forgiveness is that it keeps you in the present by letting go of the past.

Chapter Ten

Clue # 8
Practice Some Form of Meditation.

Early the next morning Charmaine walked with eager anticipation toward the waterfall for her meditation. William stood on the path below, marveling at the morning light on the flowers and watching couples strolling amiably into the day. A couple of small children played frisbee with a large, tail-wagging black lab.

"Hello, my friend," Charmaine said warmly as she approached William.

"Hi, Charmaine."

"You look uncommonly pleased with yourself this morning. Any particular reason?"

William sighed happily.

"Emily is really nice."

"Ah, Emily!"

"It's just so easy to talk to her. She actually wanted to hear what I had to say! And I loved listening to her, too. We talked for a long time...and laughed together, Charmaine!"

"That's important, isn't it?"

"I'd forgotten how good it feels to be close to someone like that. We're going for a hike this afternoon. I want to show her the lagoon and the waterfall. I feel excited and peaceful at the same time. Am I going wacko?"

"Probably," said Charmaine, with a seasoned smile. "But it's a good kind of wacko. Just keep exhaling, softening - letting go of tightness anywhere in your body. And of course, keep being honest. You'll be fine."

"You going anywhere in particular?" William asked.

"I was headed to the waterfall for my morning meditation. This would be a good time to show you how to get started. Do you have time now?"

"I do. Let's go," said William. "I've heard you talk a lot about meditation but I'm not sure what it actually is or how to do it."

"All the clues are important," Charmaine said as they turned to take the path to the waterfall, "but in many ways it's perhaps the most important one because the practical wisdom from all the other Clues can be accessed through meditation."

"Well, I imagine that makes meditation pretty much an essential skill to learn, then."

"I think so," said Charmaine. "All the others are Clues of *understanding*. And with *practice,* you develop an awareness of their value - to see how they change your experience of life for the better. On the other hand, meditation is a Clue of *practice*. It's something you practice every day and then you begin to *understand* how it can positively affect your life."

"How long does it typically take," asked William, "to understand enough to benefit from meditation?"

"Good news. You don't need to understand meditation in order to do it or for it to produce positive results in your life. If you do it, you'll come to understand its value. Meditation is an ongoing practice but the benefits will begin to come immediately. Have faith, William."

"Faith? Is meditation anything like prayer?"

"Yes, it can be. Some people think of meditation as listening to God and prayer as *talking* to God. For some people prayer is a form of meditation. Prayer and meditation can help free us from the negative effects of our ego's fearful and judgmental thoughts. Both prayer and meditation are a very personal experience."

"I'm anxious to take a shot at meditation! Oh, but maybe I should wait until I'm not so distracted by thoughts of Emily," William said with a roguish grin.

"Being distracted is not really a problem. It's just one of the possible states our 'little mind' is in sometimes. Most of us have never really given our 'little mind' much thought. It is a bit like a mischievous little child demanding all the attention it can get. It takes time and patience to train it to behave in certain ways. I think you'll be able to handle distractions just fine. It just takes practice."

"I'll have to take your word for it."

"You'll discover many of the more subtle aspects of meditation for yourself as you develop a daily practice. But for now, let's go over the basics to get you started."

"Meditation 101?"

"Yep, a little background," Charmaine said cheerfully. Although it's much more common in the East, millions in the West meditate too. Meditation is the single most direct way that I know of to bring you to opening your heart and living your life from your soul rather than from your ego. Physicians, mental health counselors, professional organizations and researchers increasingly recommend its practice. And so do I," she added with a smile.

"That's reassuring."

"It also helps reduce anxiety and depression. Did you know that meditation can also decrease blood pressure?" asked Charmaine.

"I didn't," William said. "My blood pressure has risen quite a bit since I started this job. Maybe meditating will help me bring it down."

Charmaine listed more benefits of meditation on her fingers.

"Meditation also allows deep rest, helps eliminate tension and fatigue, and increases mental clarity - which, by the way, would also contribute to improving your performance at work."

"Those sound like the benefits of regular exercise."

"Yes, and similarly, you are not likely to see remarkable results after just one workout. But over time you begin to see a cumulative effect from a regular practice. And just like those who exercise daily, those who meditate regularly will find their mind becoming more agile, sharper, stronger, more clear and finally more peaceful."

"More peaceful, huh?"

"Tempting, isn't it," Charmaine said with a grin. "People who meditate are usually less anxious and tend to view life in a more positive way. Meditation actually helps develop a more friendly and open attitude."

"Oh, good! It'll make me a nicer person," said William.

"If that's possible," she said sincerely. "And every once in a while, you may have what feels like a very special meditation."

"*How* special?"

"Sometimes you get to a place where you become aware of a very deep calmness, clarity and sense of timeless peace."

"Sounds nice."

"It is. There's a very thin veil between the physical and the spiritual realms. Meditation can take you through that veil to the place where the soul resides. Here's the heart of the matter: *All suffering comes from forming attachments. All our attachments are formed by thoughts. Meditation is the moment-to-moment practice of letting go of the attachments formed by those thoughts. Meditation is the single most powerful practice that can help free me from fear and suffering.*"

"I thought the purpose of meditation was to quiet the mind."

"Some would tell you that's its purpose, but I think that's an incorrect approach and a tragic mistake if we consider the potential benefits of more people meditating. That false assumption is the main reason most people don't meditate. They can't quiet their minds."

"My mind is incessantly thinking, planning, worrying - making judgments. I don't think I could ever stop its buzzing and chattering."

"Well, here's good news. Although quieting the mind is not at all the *purpose* of meditation, it can be an occasional and wonderful outcome of it."

"Not only that, but if we take the position that the purpose of meditation is to quiet the mind, we automatically set up an adversarial relationship with our 'little-mind'."

"Let the war begin, right?"

"Exactly. That kind of opposition doesn't come from the soul. Opposition comes from fear, from our ego. That's why we don't want to unwittingly make our 'little-mind', with all its incessant 'busyness' and clever tricks, the enemy."

"I get enough opposition in life without adding to it from the inside," said William.

"That's why in meditation it's important to *lovingly* notice your thoughts, rather than push them away, as a controlling adversary might do. On the other hand, it's also why we don't hold onto them like a clingy, attached ego might do. The *loving witness within* simply allows thoughts to flow through our awareness."

"I trust that comes with practice for thick-skinned guys like me?"

"Remember, your mind thinks it is you and that its very survival depends on staying in control. The way it tries to stay in control is by thinking its thoughts. Your mind doesn't want to give up its illusion of control and will do anything to prevent it."

"Like finding perfectly good reasons not to meditate?"

"Yes, and if you tell your mind you're going to teach it something that will quiet it..."

"... *my* mind would say, 'Yeah, you and who else?'"

They both laughed.

"So in meditation," William recapped, "I needn't bother attempting to quiet my mind. I just practice being a compassionate *witness* to it?"

Charmaine nodded, waiting for him to go on.

"...and rather than trying to *quiet* my mind, meditation is more about understanding that I am *not* my mind."

"Good job, William! That's why in meditation you don't push thoughts away nor do you hold onto them."

"What's left to do then?"

"You lovingly notice them and return your attention to your breath, and a focus point such as a visual object, a physical movement or a word."

"A *focus* word?"

"I'll explain when we get to a place where we can practice," said Charmaine. "We're nearly to the waterfall."

"Thoughts are the mechanism," she continued, "that the mind uses to create its experience of the world. In a sense our unseen thoughts - our attitudes, beliefs and assumptions - create the lens through which we view the world. They create all the *meaning* we add to the world's neutral facts and events."

"Then nothing has meaning except the meaning we give it..."

"That's right, William. Thoughts create our day-to-day experience of life. Remember: *the world is just out there worlding. Whatever we experience is what we bring to it.*"

"So these peaceful thoughts I'm having right now are actually creating my experience of the world while its just out there *worlding*?"

"Some would be bored or even anxious in this same scenario. It's all in our perception of it."

"The world doesn't *feel* like it's *out there*. Right now, it feels like I'm a *part* of it."

"That *thought* is creating your sense of connectedness with the world," Charmaine said. "*You* are really the source of your own experience, not the world. We all are. The world *is* out there *worlding*, it's true, *but how each of us experiences it is determined by the meaning we each give it."*

William stopped in his tracks, a still-life of open-mouthed amazement.

"My God! If that's true... that means... do you realize what that *means*?" he stammered in stunned realization. "If I got good at letting go of attachments formed by my fear-based thoughts, my old negative patterns of thinking and feeling would change - or even disappear!"

"Now you begin to see why meditation can be so powerful in affecting the quality of your life," Charmaine said quietly. "At least you won't be as likely to give your ego more power to run your life than your soul. *You'll* have your negative thoughts instead of *them* having you. All those negative thoughts are not likely to go away entirely. But over time you'll notice they become a little less interesting. Does that make sense to you?""

"Yeah, it sure does... because *I'm not my mind or my thoughts.* I'm the *witness* to my thoughts."

"In a sense, you'll be learning to lovingly relate to your own mind and its thoughts rather than fearfully relating *from* them. That's when everything begins to change. That's when you begin to reclaim ownership of the quality of your own life. Otherwise you'd be like a wind sock: 'How are you feeling?' 'I don't know - which way is the wind blowing?'"

They laughed, as they entered the clearing beneath the falls. Standing silently for a moment, they admired its towering majesty. Nearby flowers glistened with a light mist.

"It's hard to believe this glorious setting isn't creating the way I feel right now, as I stand here soaking up its energy and beauty," William said, drawing deep breaths of fresh sunlit air. "I sure don't feel like this when I'm stuck in a crowded freeway!"

"Settings can enhance meditative states," said Charmaine. "But the setting is not all of it. Our state of mind in each moment also has a lot to do with it. There are indeed natural settings - and even the presence of certain people - that make it easier to open our hearts and see the world through more loving, compassionate eyes. Remember how you felt earlier while watching the little children playing?"

"Sure..."

"For most of us, babies are so full of love that fearful and negative thoughts have a hard time getting a grip on our minds while in their presence. Remember, *the power of an open heart is that a closed heart cannot stay closed in its presence.* For most of us, young ones and natural settings like the ocean, mountains, and this waterfall tend to soothe and refresh our spirits."

"They seem to take less energy to be around," William agreed. "In fact, they're an energizing influence."

"It's not news to you that there are some places and people that take a lot of energy to be around, that drain your energy."

"How would you put it? 'Soul-robbing'?" said William.

"Yes, *soul-robbing.*"

"Like it used to be with my boss. It took a lot of energy to be around him. I used to feel tired just thinking about having to see him. But it doesn't take as much energy now. I guess he's just been out there 'bossing'. Lately, I think I've been naturally reclaiming the power I was giving *him* to determine the quality of *my* life. And you know what? He's not so bad."

"Good, William! You're beginning to experience the practical value of the Clues. To truly understand the power of meditation is to understand the power of love."

"I don't get the connection."

"Love is your true state of being. The thoughts your 'little-mind' has are what take you out of that natural loving state of being. There's therefore nothing you have to do *to be* in your loving self. It's who you really are - always there waiting for you to come back to it. You only have to *undo* what took you *out* of our loving state in the first place. It's the moment-to-moment practice of lovingly letting go of the attachments formed by your little mind's fearful, insecure thoughts that allow you to spontaneously come back to your deeper, loving self. Meditation is about identifying with your soul rather than with your ego."

"How can I do that?"

"You don't have to *do* that. It's simply the way you're *wired-up* - the way you're designed. That's why meditation is so helpful. Like a softening breath, it's a *path* to your center, to your soul. Think of it this way. You don't have to do anything to make the sun shine. But sometimes you have to get free of the clouds in order to experience the light."

"I hope it's easy..."

"It's very simple, but not necessarily easy."

"Well, Charmaine, I'm a practical guy. How do I do it?"

"Let's sit here on this bench, William, and we'll go over the basic steps to meditating. There are four."

"Okay," he said , settling himself comfortably.

Meditation: Step One

"The first step is to find a comfortable place to meditate - like right here. Choose a peaceful place away from phones, pagers, the TV, radio - any sort of distraction. This is most important when you're first learning. Later, as you develop the skill, it's desirable but less necessary. Eventually you'll find you can meditate anytime and anywhere. As you develop your own meditation practice, you'll probably be inclined to do it at the same time and in the same place every day. Setting aside 15 to 20 minutes twice a day is ideal. But remember, it's more important *that* you meditate, than *where* or *how long* you do it.

Meditation: Step Two

"Second, your posture is important."

William pulled his shoulders back and sat up a little.

"That's right. Sit up straight so your backbone is vertical and your head is upright. This is ideal but it's more important that you're comfortable. If you're not comfortable, your 'little-mind' will simply use it as an excuse not to meditate at all."

"How's this?"

"You're leaning a little and your chin is drooping. I believe it's important to be symmetrical in your sitting position, rather than leaning one way or another. I personally have noticed that it's easier to be spiritually centered when my body is centered."

"Seems logical," William murmured as he readjusted his weight on the bench.

Meditation: Step Three

"The third step is to close your eyes."

William closed his eyes.

"Take a few moments. Now soften your eyes, your tongue and your belly."

"No problem with softening my belly," William said, chuckling as he followed her instructions.

"Then you lovingly begin to watch your breath."

"*Watch* my breath?"

"Yes, gently follow your breathing," said Charmaine. "Feel your breath come in and go out of your body. *Become your breath. Let it have you.* I know that may sound a little strange right now but as you develop your meditation practice, even after only a few weeks, it will make more sense. You may soon notice that you don't *have* to breathe at all. You can simply begin to lovingly notice what it feels like to allow your body to breathe itself. It knows how to do that just fine without any help from you. There really is nothing for you to *do*. Just *be* that loving observer, a gentle witness to your thoughts and awarenesses. It's like sitting on a train and passively watching the scenery go by. *Lovingly noticing* is your soul smiling at your ego with all its thought-filled distractions and saying, 'That's okay. Let's just let the thoughts go for now. We can come back to them later if you still want to.'"

"Okay, I'm not my mind and I'm not my body. So I *lovingly* notice my body breathing itself. What about all these unrelated thoughts flitting around right now? Should I lovingly *notice* my mind thinking those thoughts, too?"

"That's exactly right," said Charmaine quietly. "The next part of this step is to choose a short word or phrase to use as a *soulful point of focus* as you breathe."

"That must be the *focus word*," he said, looking a little uncomfortable.

"Choose a simple one, something that helps you identify with your soul rather than your *ego*."

"I don't even know where to start..."

"You can use any word that helps you connect with your deeper self. Like 'love', 'peace', 'joy', 'one', 'om'..."

"Hmmm."

"Some Christians use the word 'Jesus'. Some Buddhists use the word 'Buddha'. Some Hindus use the phrase 'Hong-Sau'. Some Muslims use the word 'Allah'. Some Jewish people use the word 'Shalom'. It really doesn't matter. One of my dear old friends says 'wave'. For her, God is like the ocean and she is a wave. Her life represents her unique journey that eventually takes her to the shore and back into the One. Any word that helps you connect with your deeper self will work fine."

"How about 'clappernoseflight'," William suggested, chuckling.

"Try to keep it to one or two syllables," Charmaine said, smiling. "It's simply for a soulful point of focus, but if 'clappernoseflight' helps you connect with your deeper self, go for it."

"I'll have to give it some thought," said William more seriously. "Tell me again how it'll help me meditate?"

"You say it each time you exhale. Your focus word is your secondary point of focus. Your breath is the primary point of focus. Continually refocusing on your breath and your word are simply a way to lovingly bring your attention to the moment. Bring your attention back to your breath whenever you become aware that you have a thought and your attention has strayed. As you get comfortable watching your breath, begin to meditate by quietly saying your focus word with each exhalation. This can be done silently in your mind or as a quiet whisper."

Meditation: Step Four

"Now here's the tricky part," continued Charmaine. "The fourth step is to take an absolutely loving, unconditionally accepting attitude toward this *soulful-activity* we call meditation. Remember you can't do it wrong. Whenever you become aware of having a thought while meditating, gently notice you had that thought, no matter what it is, and return all your awareness to your breath and your focus word on the next exhalation. If you're annoyed or discouraged that a stray thought crept in, then *lovingly* notice you just had that critical thought and return your attention to your breath and your focus word. No matter what happens while meditating, *lovingly* notice it and return your attention to your breath. And as you exhale, quietly say your focus word."

"Keep in mind that your mind thinks it is you and thinks its survival depends on staying in control. So it will do anything it can to persuade you not to meditate. In a way, your ego mistakes meditation for nonexistence or death."

"So can I try it right now?"

Charmaine smiled at William's impatience to 'patiently' meditate.

"Well, William, not really…"

"No?"

"Meditation doesn't involve *trying*. It's about just *being*. But I know what you meant," she laughed, "and we can certainly meditate for a bit and then talk about it, if you like."

"I'm ready!"

"Remember, you can only meditate or not meditate. And if you do meditate, you couldn't do it wrong even if you wanted to."

"That's good to know."

"I've meditated thousands of times and each time is different. My *mind* would tell you that some meditations were better than others. But the *reality* is that each was a perfect reflection of my state of being in that moment. Conclusion?" She waited expectantly for his response.

"Can't screw it up! Gotcha," said William quickly.

"So let's give it a … go."

Charmaine moved to a grassy spot beneath a nearby tree, crossed her legs, yoga-style, resting her upturned palms in her lap, closed her eyes and drew a long, slow breath. She 'softened'. William sat down beside her, straightened his back with his head resting comfortably upright. He wiggled around a little until he got comfortable.

"How's this?"

Charmaine glanced over at William. She smiled at his sincerity. "Good. Now close your eyes, *soften* and begin to bring all your loving attention to your breath. Remember, choose a focus word to say each time you exhale - one that helps you connect with your deeper self."

He closed his eyes, *softened* as Charmaine had explained, and began to 'watch' his breath. It felt good. Then he became aware of the sound of the waterfall. It amazed him that for a few moments before, he'd been completely unaware of it! How could he have been unaware of a sound that close? Then he realized that he hadn't decided on a focus word. At first, he thought 'peaceful' would be good, but then 'free' also had a nice ring to it. He had been struggling with which word to use for several minutes and lost track of his breath.

"Damn," he thought. "I've already messed this up. No," he reminded himself. "Charmaine said I can't do it wrong; I can only do it or not do it. I just need practice. My ego would do anything to distract me from meditation. Ah ha! That's what's happening right now!"

William felt a twinge of compassion for his 'little mind' which was earnestly working its usual control strategy.

"That's okay, little guy," he chuckled inwardly, "we'll just choose the word 'peaceful' for now."

And he brought his attention back to his breath for the first time since they started. As William exhaled he silently thought 'peaceful'. He continued to 'watch' his breath and as he exhaled he repeated his focus word.

"Hey, I think I'm getting the hang of this! Charmaine was right about my 'little mind' trying to distract me. Maybe this won't take a lot of tedious practice after all..."

Then he realized that a couple more minutes had passed and again, he had not 'watched' his breath nor had he used his focus word. He tenderly laughed to himself. "Well, you slippery little bugger! I can see this is going to be a bit trickier than I thought."

Once again William returned his attention to his breath and as he exhaled he thought 'peaceful'. He continued like this for a while and was feeling just fine when he realized his butt itched. He squirmed a little, but it didn't stop the itch. William didn't know what to do so he kept 'watching' his breath. Yet he couldn't help thinking about his rear-end itching.

"I sure would like to be free of this itch," he thought. "And I'm still not sure which word is really the best for me." Then he noticed that the itch had disappeared from his awareness and he thought surely that was a sign that he should use the word 'free' rather than 'peaceful' for his focus word. He thought about how enlightened he must be to have intuited that wisdom. Once again, William realized that he had not been 'watching' his breath or saying his focus word. And once again, he gently brought his attention back to his breath, thinking 'free' as he exhaled.

"Yes," William thought happily, "that feels right. 'Free' is clearly a better word... but I do like 'peaceful' too... maybe I should make a list and... damn! I'm doing it again," he thought with intense exasperation. "Charmaine," he said aloud. "Can we talk for a few minutes?"

She gently brought her attention to her friend, anticipating the struggles all beginners typically experience.

"Of course, William. What's on your mind?"

"You mean my 'little mind', don't you," he muttered. "How long was that, Charmaine? It felt like forever."

"Well, actually it was about five minutes."

William rolled onto his back and laughed.

"Are you kidding? It seemed like a big chunk of my entire life all rolled up into a small package. I went through self-doubt, confusion, impatience, flip-flopping, putting myself down, and even *spiritual pride,* if you can imagine that! That's exactly the way I've been at work much of the time. Geez! Is that what meditation is - a micro-cosm of my life?"

"Yes, it is. Sometimes it is, but it's okay. Pretty soon you'll get famil-iar with your ego's favorite tricks for avoiding being fully present."

"I couldn't stay focused more than a few moments at a time before my mind raced in and did everything from beat me up to compli-ment me on what a good meditator I am!"

"It gets easier," she assured him, "easier to return to your breath and your focus word. If that seemed like a long time to you, remem-ber it's just one of your ego's illusions to distract you from meditating. Soon, you'll have time when the minutes seem to fly. Even an hour can seem like only a short time. In deep meditation you'll discover that time is not linear but relative. There is only a sense of *being.*"

"In twenty-five words or less," William said, scratching his head, "draw me a picture of what that is like, so I'll recognize it – if I ever get there..."

"This is not a magical experience and it's not a place where you ar-rive. It's found in any moment free of anxiety and fear. We all spend more time in this state of being than we may realize. Meditation is simply a way to deepen and cultivate a state of being that is natural to all of us. It's found in those moments of peacefulness, tranquility and calm that occasionally occur in our lives."

"I probably do have more of those moments than I tend to realize. It's just that those bad feelings used to take up most of my day. So tell me Charmaine, what word do you use for your point of focus?

"I use the word 'one' for my meditation. It came out of a moment in meditation many years ago. In that moment I saw that *I was one with all that is.* So the word 'one' has a very powerful centering effect for me. And yet, I occasionally hear a little voice while I meditate that says, 'One? Why one? Wouldn't 'two' be twice as good?' Or I'll see little 'ones' flying by with beautiful little wings..."

"*You* get distracted during meditation, even now?"

"Sure. My mind will do whatever it can to distract me. Remember, your ego is not the enemy. It's innocent but misguided. Sometimes I'll get an itch. It's just one more attempt by my ego to stay in control."

"That happened to me! All of a sudden my butt itched."

"So what did you do?"

"Well, after a bit it just seemed to disappear. I was thinking about wanting to be 'free' of the itch. This confused things because I really couldn't decide between the words 'peaceful' and 'free' Then I realized I hadn't been 'watching' my breath or using either 'peaceful' or 'free' as a focus word. My mind had just taken me on another ramble."

"Sometimes I get an itch or a kink in my leg, too," Charmaine said. "I consider any distracting physical awareness as a 'body thought'. So, I just lovingly notice I have that awareness, as with any other thought, and bring my attention back to my breath, saying 'one' as I exhale. If it happens again, I do the same thing again."

"What if it won't go away?"

"I usually scratch the itch or stretch the leg and rub it for a moment. Then I simply return my attention to my breath and lovingly say 'one' as I exhale. The idea here is not to set up an adversarial relationship with your mind/body, the ego structure."

"Kill it with kindness, huh?" William grinned.

"Not really. It's a matter of loving its innocence. That automatically helps us identify with our soul rather than with our ego in that moment. Anyway, if you're not reasonably comfortable, it's not likely you'll continue to practice."

"True. I'm a 'comfort' kind of guy," he agreed.

"You may be aware of how often I use the phrase 'lovingly notice'."

"Yeah, I 'lovingly noticed' it," said William.

Charmaine liked William's emerging sense of humor. She smiled appreciatively and continued.

"Lovingly noticing is important because meditation is not a neutral activity. And it's certainly not an adversarial one. It a *soulful* activity. The soul, the loving witness within, is not neutral and it's not adversarial. It's actively loving, patient, merciful and compassionate. So you see, the soul does not *just* notice. It '*lovingly*' notices."

"I see the distinction," he said with sudden comprehension. "The *ego* would just *notice* or more accurately, *judge*, while the *soul* would 'lovingly notice'. That is an important difference!"

"It's not just an important difference. It is an essential difference."

"What about changing my focus word in mid-meditation? Was that okay?

"At one level, nothing you do in meditation is 'not okay'. But generally I wouldn't change my focus word in midstream. My 'little mind' has invited me to do that many times. Dealing with your own ego is a little like dealing with an innocent but tenacious and mischievous child."

"Uh-oh!" William grimaced as he thought of his own 'inner child', or was it 'inner children'? Yikes.

"But when you're not meditating," said Charmaine, "feel free to think about it and experiment. See which word or phrase feels right. As you first develop your practice, there are many things you'll undoubtedly personalize for yourself. Eventually, you'll begin to settle into a way that feels comfortable. Remember, it's more important that you meditate than how you meditate."

"When I was trying to... oops... I mean when I was meditating, I noticed a familiar pattern to the distractions," he mused. "They were pretty much just like the rest of my life, especially at work."

"You've just touched on the very heart of why meditation is the most powerful and practical tool you can use to improve the quality of your life! We all have what I call sub-personalities. These are different facets of our ego structure. And, no, it doesn't mean we're all 'schizo'," Charmaine added as William opened his mouth to make a wisecrack.

"I'm glad to hear that."

"There's nothing wrong with these *sub-personalities* or roles we play in this life. They really are wonderful parts of who we are. For example, in me I see a mother, a little girl, an athlete, an artist/musician, a dancer, a teacher/coach, a passionate lover and an old spiritual seeker. These are all fine aspects of my being. But when my heart closes and I'm in a reactive state, these aspects of me will use all their methods to try to stay in control."

"I understand the concept of different roles all rolled up in one person. But are we really all possessed by a gaggle of naughty sub-personalities who are constantly trying to control us?" William asked, perplexed. "That sounds somewhat daunting - even a little scary!"

"They are all wonderful aspects of your being, William. When your heart is open and you're coming from love, your soulful presence is manifested through these various parts in wonderful ways such as patience, playfulness, tenacity, curiosity, and creativity. When your heart is closed and you're coming from fear, they manifest in ways that negatively affect the quality of your life, such as impatience, rigidness, stuckness, arrogance and boredom."

"This is a very important point, William. In fact, it's the reason meditation is the single most effective thing you can do to enhance the quality of your life. Your ego uses a vast array of tricks and distractions in order to try to stay in control in your every day life. During meditation it will use all the same strategies to get you not to meditate. So, in aggregate and over time, when you meditate you will have the *inescapable* opportunity to face and move through all of your ego's favorite controlling, fear-based thoughts."

"Illustration, please," said William.

"For example, if one of your sub-personalities tends to get bored easily, meditation will bore you to tears. If a part of you tends to get a little cocky or arrogant, you might begin to think you're so good at meditating you don't need to do it anymore. If part of you tends to get angry easily, you may initially find meditation irritating. If another part tends to be critical and self-deprecating, you might think you're so lousy at meditating you may as well not bother. If a part of you tends to get lots of bellyaches or headaches, meditation might initially also give you a bellyache or a headache. If one part never seems to have enough time, it will try to convince you that you don't have time to meditate. Our sub-personalities' 'little minds' are very clever and more than a little slippery at staying in control. They've had years of practice!"

"My God! You've just described my inner rabble to a tee!"

"It's really not such a mystery. We all have a similar crowd running around inside us."

"So then, what's your practical, do-it-yourself secret of *crowd control*?"

"I believe the practical value of meditation is this: if we meditate through all these attempted *takeovers*, through all the tendencies our various sub-personalities use to try to control our lives, we'll begin to see them retreat and *become less interesting.*"

"That would be nice..."

"And here's the ultimate clincher, the practical power of meditation. The fear based thoughts don't just begin to disappear or become less interesting in your meditation; they eventually stop showing up *in your everyday life.*

"Meditation isn't intended to solve all of life's problems, though it does tend to give us a larger perspective from which to bring our best resources to manage those problems."

"For example, Charmaine?"

"You may notice in your everyday life that you begin to take things a little less seriously, without losing passion in your activities. You may notice you begin to take things less personally even when someone is right in your face. You may notice you are listening better and are more able to set boundaries and to ask for what you want. You may notice your intuition and your creativity are available more often. Because meditation is a practice that cultivates being present in the moment, you may notice your sense of taste, touch, smell and sound are heightened. These are only a few of the many benefits of meditation. And most importantly, there is no other single activity that will bring you more directly to your soul. Meditation creates an inescapable opportunity to move through all the fear-based patterns in your life. And all you have to do is *do it!* You can't even do it wrong. You can only do it or not do it. It simply works."

"Thank you, Charmaine. You've given me a great gift!"

"Believe me, William, sharing with you has been a gift for me as well. We're both blessed."

Summary

Clue #8:
Practice Some Form of Meditation

Meditation is the single most powerful practice that can help free ourselves from fear and suffering. All suffering comes from the ego forming attachments. All attachments are formed by thoughts. Meditation is the moment-to-moment practice of letting go of the attachments formed by those thoughts. Meditation can take many forms. Find what works best for you. It simply works. We can only do it or not do it. We can't even do it wrong. Ultimately, the purpose of meditation is to help us identify with our soul rather than with our ego.

- All suffering comes from forming attachments. All our attachments are formed by thoughts. Meditation is the moment-to-moment practice of letting go of the attachments formed by those thoughts.

- The purpose of meditation is not to quiet the mind. It is to lovingly understand that you are not your mind. Be a compassionate witness to it.

- Meditation has a cumulative effect. The benefits accrue over time.

- Meditation is about identifying with your soul rather than with your ego.

- Meditation is not intended to solve all of life's problems. But it does tend to give you a bigger perspective from which you can bring the best of your resources to manage and deal with those situations.

- You can only meditate or not meditate. And if you do meditate, you can't do it wrong even if you wanted to. Even if you meditate thousands of times each time is different. Your mind will tell you that some meditations are better than others. But the reality is that each is a perfect reflection of your state of being in that moment.

Meditation

Step One: Find a comfortable and peaceful place to meditate. As you develop your own meditation practice, you may feel inclined to do it at the same time and in the same place every day. 15 to 20 minutes twice a day is ideal. But it is more important *that* you do it, rather than *where* or *how long* you do it.

Step Two: Posture is important. Sit up straight so your backbone is vertical and your head is upright. This is ideal but it's more important that you're comfortable. It's important to be symmetrical in your sitting position, rather than leaning one way or another. It's easier to be spiritually centered when your body is centered.

Step Three: Close your eyes and soften your eyes, your tongue and your belly. 'Lovingly' begin to watch your breath. Feel your breath come in and go out of your body. *Become your breath. Let it have you.* Just *be* that loving observer, a gentle witness to your thoughts and awarenesses. It's like sitting on a train and passively watching the scenery go by. Then choose a short word or phrase as a *soulful point of focus* to accompany your breathing. Try to keep it to one or two syllables. Say it each time you exhale. Your focus word is your secondary point of focus. Your breath is the primary point of focus. Your breath and your word are simply ways to 'lovingly' bring your attention to the moment. As you get comfortable watching your breath, begin to meditate by quietly saying your focus word to yourself with each exhalation. This can be done silently in your mind or as a quiet whisper. Bring your attention back to your breath whenever you become aware that you have a thought and your attention has strayed.

Step Four: Take an absolutely loving, unconditionally accepting attitude toward this 'soulful-activity' we call meditation. You cannot do it wrong. Whenever you become aware of having a thought while meditating, 'lovingly' notice you had that thought - no matter what it is - and gently return all your awareness to your breath and your focus word on the next exhalation. If you're annoyed or discouraged or critical that a stray thought crept in, then just 'lovingly' notice you had *that* thought and gently return your attention to your breath and your focus word. No matter what happens while meditating, *lovingly* notice it and return your attention to your breath. And as you exhale, quietly say your focus word.

Sub-Personalities

We all have what might be called sub-personalities. These are different facets of our ego structure. There is nothing wrong with these sub-personalities. They are wonderful aspects of who we are. But when our heart closes and we're in a reactive state, these aspects will use all their methods to try to stay in control. The practical value of meditation is that if we meditate through all these attempted 'takeovers', through all the tendencies our various sub-personalities use to try to stay in control, we'll begin to see them retreat and become *less interesting*. They don't just begin to disappear or become less interesting in our meditation – they eventually stop showing up *in our everyday life*. Meditation creates a constant opportunity to move through all the fear-based patterns in our life. This is ultimately the practical power of meditation.

The Benefits of Meditation

- Meditation decreases blood pressure.

- It helps reduce anxiety and mild to moderate depression.

- Meditation allows deep rest, helps eliminate tension and fatigue, and increases mental clarity.

- If you meditate regularly you will find your mind becoming more agile, sharper, stronger, more clear and finally more peaceful.

- You will find you are less anxious and tend to view life in a more positive way.

- It actually helps develop a more friendly and open attitude.

- You may start to notice in your everyday life that you begin to take things a little less seriously, without loosing passion in your activities.

- You may notice you begin to take things less personally even when someone is right in your face.

- You may notice you are listening better and are more able to set boundaries and to ask for what you want.

- You may notice your intuition and your creativity are available more of the time.

- Because meditation is a practice that cultivates being present in the moment, you may notice your sense of taste, touch, smell and sound are heightened.

Chapter Eleven

Epilogue

Completing the Circle

One evening William sat on a boulder by the bridge where he and Charmaine had often stood overlooking the city. The world, as it had been then, was still just out there *worlding*. He hadn't seen Charmaine for several years. She was off on another leg of her journey.

"It's an inward journey, William," she had said with a cryptic grin. "But sometimes you have to go away to do it."

He supposed that's what he had unknowingly done by moving to this city from his home town. He remembered Charmaine laughing and saying, "Geographical escape doesn't work, except when it does."

William missed her laughter and her loving presence.

He missed her gentle coaching on the Eight Clues. Missing Charmaine gave him plenty of practice in letting go of attachment - his attachment to her. It caused him to realize at a more profound level that the answers in life never really lie outside one's deeper self. That's what Charmaine meant about life being an inward journey.

In attending to his own spiritual life and practices, William studied many different traditions. Once again, he found himself enjoying visiting places of worship, because for him they were places to celebrate life. He discovered that the essence of religion was based in the same spirituality, that virtually all religions of the world believe that access to the Divine lies *within*. This comforted William as he faced the ever-changing landscape of his own life.

Much had changed in William's life during Charmaine's absence. He reconnected with his family and had visited them several times. He continued practicing forgiveness toward his father. He truly enjoyed seeing his mother with her loving smile he had so missed. It reminded William of Charmaine in some comforting way. He caught up on all the things that were going on with his brother and sister – which included meeting her new baby girl – Uncle William's little angel.

On a recent fly fishing trip with his dad, William shared much of what was going on in his life and what he had learned from Charmaine, especially about forgiveness. His father appreciated how William was able to *tell on himself* and apologize for his contribution to the problems in their relationship. He was amazed how strong William seemed, and completely free of anger or defensiveness. And William seemed genuinely interested in what was happening in his life. His boy had done some serious growing. He was proud of him. And he liked him.

In the presence of William's open-heartedness his father was able to acknowledge that he now knew he had not really been there for his kids when they most needed him. He admitted he just didn't know how to be a real father at the time and so he'd stayed focused on his work, letting Mom raise the kids. He was finally able to begin accepting and forgiving himself, realizing it wasn't too late to build a strong, loving relationship with his growing family.

William had let go of his unrealistic attachment to needing his father to be perfect. He began to see his father as a man, like himself, with strengths and faults and with challenges and shortcomings.

William began to understand that he'd never even considered what his dad *had* provided for him, in addition to all the pressures and expectations his father must have been under. True, as a father image, he had failed them in many ways. But as a man, he had simply done the best he knew at the time.

William came to feel much more compassion for his own personal struggles and shortcomings. (Charmaine said it was easier to forgive others if we first forgive ourselves.) That realization helped him feel more compassionate and generous toward *himself*. It was a delightfully circular experience. It amazed William how letting go of his attachment to what he *had not* received from his father was just as liberating as letting go of his attachment to what he *had* received from Charmaine!

Sitting quietly one afternoon William experienced a moment of deep joy while reflecting on a question Charmaine had posed to him.

"What if you took the position that we each attract, like magnets, at the moment of our conception and for each moment of our entire life, the very circumstances and people we each need? What if we did this in order to create for ourselves an inescapable opportunity to face the next issue we are ready to face along our spiritual journey? Would it change how you felt about your life if you knew you had actually participated in choosing your very existence, your parents, your time, place and country of origin, your race, your sex and your genetic conditions?"

To William, the implication of this was huge. What if there is a meaning in everything and everything occurs for a reason? What if our life is somehow predisposed, the grand paradox being that we also have free will to deal with each predisposition, moment-to-moment? What if the universe is unfolding exactly as it must and is a constant reflection of the choices we each make? And what if, in aggregate, the world we all live in is also a perfect reflection of the choices we each make?

Then William realized it didn't really matter if it were true or not. If he simply *took the position* that it was true, he felt incredibly freed, supported and empowered by life rather than victimized by the facts and circumstances of his youth and his adulthood. It was a very powerful frame shift.

He and Emily had gotten much closer, too. In fact, he was getting ready to ask her to marry him. He could be more open and honest with Emily than he had ever been with anyone. William enjoyed the feeling of transparency in their relationship. It helped him feel authentic and available for intimacy, and though sometimes risky, it felt both freeing and energizing to be so open. Now he could share thoughts and feelings with Emily that he used to keep hidden in order to appear strong and not so vulnerable. It seemed strange that it was just the opposite.

William was gradually becoming stronger and less fearful. He had found his backbone and discovered it was not rigid or mean-spirited! He loved Emily and realized he had more than ever to bring to a relationship. He was learning to talk to her with an open heart, with an intention to simply share rather than justify himself or convince her to see things his way. He felt safe enough to listen so she felt heard and understood, rather than respond too quickly or contradict her.

William no longer felt responsible for the quality of other people's lives. He respected Emily's natural ability to solve her own problems. He had learned to be more patient and to ask her what he could do, or how he could be, that would actually cause her to feel supported by him. He could be compassionate with Emily when she was down or struggling, without taking it on as his own issue. He'd learned how to be fully present with her without getting enmeshed and entangled in her life *and* without going away from her. It was very liberating for both of them.

Fear of conflict had ceased to be a problem since William had come to see it as a natural part of life. He now saw it as a positive, creative part of any relationship as long as he was honest and open-hearted rather than adversarial. All these skills also applied to relationships with friends, family, community activities and at work. Life was definitely getting better for William.

His work life had been transformed. A large multinational corporation bought out his company. His boss and most of the other managers and employees were initially scared, suspicious and angry. Cutbacks and out-sourcing concerned everyone there. And indeed, some employees were forced out and were suffering.

However, William had learned to embrace change. He now had increasing trust in the Universe. He wasn't entirely clear where things were headed but he had decided he would play a positive role in directing the course of those changes.

It turned out that the new leadership of the company was not initially as open and interested as he had hoped. They had some excellent ideas about possible new directions for the company but showed little interest in what the employees had to say. They also were reluctant to be open to revealing their bigger intentions.

In the face of all the angst and despair, his boss noticed William's positive stance toward the future of the company and enlisted his support for himself and the other managers. William helped create a forum for people to talk about what they were feeling and to be more present to their own fears and concerns. William learned that what employees really want from their work is job satisfaction and clear communication.

For his staff to feel really satisfied with their jobs, William knew they needed to be able to find meaning and value - a feeling of participation and importance to the company's over-all goals. They needed recognition and trust from the leadership. That wouldn't be easy.

Understanding that honest communication was a key to this, William found a way to help his own staff and others, including his boss, not get stuck in the past or worried about the future.

He helped them see that it was their thoughts, their attitudes and their old beliefs that actually created their moment to moment experiences, not their present circumstances. He watched them begin to tap into their natural creativity, intuition, timing and balance. This synergistic effect began to transform their worst fears into more creative and effective choices and possibilities. Over a period of time, this optimistic approach spread to other groups and departments in the company.

Eventually the new management began to be more open to its employees and started to participate by offering support. William encouraged the merging corporation to bring in people to help employees get the information they needed, to feel more secure and valued. William now actually looked forward to work and saw some new directions for himself to expand this positive influence.

There were other positive changes in his life. William and George became best friends. He enjoyed this connection and loved getting closer to George's family and his circle of friends. He realized his previous loneliness had been self-imposed. He and George run and work out three or four times a week.

William lost his extra pounds, paying attention to what he put in his body. He reads more and watches television less.

He and George joined a meditation group and took Tai Chi lessons together, which helped create a structure to support his daily spiritual practice. He discovered something very expansive about meditating and practicing Tai Chi or Yoga with others.

"I'd never think about starving my body," he thought. "So why would I allow my soul to starve?" He found meditation nurtured him to the core of his being.

William discovered that learning spiritual practices such as meditation from someone with years of experience was very helpful, maybe essential, to getting started. A classroom setting and being able to hear other people's questions and experiences helped, too. In the quiet moments of his own meditation it helped to lovingly notice his own thoughts when he was stressed. He learned to be conscious of what these thoughts tended to do to his life. William found peace and compassion when he identified with the witness deep within rather than with his fearful, reactive ego.

He also discovered, on his own, that meditation was not just one thing, that it existed on a spectrum of possible soul-nurturing experiences that might be only a few seconds or hours long, such as knitting, painting, walking or simply following the rhythmic flow of his breath. He found himself taking a centering, 'letting go' breath many times through the day, like mini-meditations.

There were other changes William began to see in his everyday life. He didn't take things so personally or quite so seriously. He felt more passion not only in his work and his relationships but also in his play and alone times. He felt more in touch with his intuition and creativity. He got back into journaling and enjoying music and photography. With Emily's playful assistance he had even begun to enjoy dancing again.

William listened better to himself and to others. He found it easier to say 'no' and to ask for what he wanted. He became more playful and more able to be present in the moment. William felt a palpable connection to the earth and an appreciation and wonder for all its creatures. Everything seemed lighter and he felt bigger. The idea that we are all connected as one was no longer theoretical, no longer just an idea. It was literal, real and evolving into a way of being for him.

Out of this growing sense of connectedness, William became more involved in his community, a giving that fed his soul. William and George began volunteering with a local service group dealing with the issues of hunger and homelessness in their community. He got his company to sponsor several of the projects. Because he loved being around kids, William started coaching a little league baseball team.

William was not yet fully aware of the positive influence of his own growing presence. Charmaine had passed something on to him, and now William was passing it on to others, just by his loving presence.

The spirituality inherent in the Eight Clues turned out to be more practical than he had first realized. And it came up everywhere in his life without necessarily talking about spirit or soul. It had everything to do with moment-to-moment everyday living of life to the fullest. The magic of being totally present boiled down to simply learning to expand, heighten and broaden his awareness and feelings of the realities of being human. William began to more fully experience wholeness with himself, others and nature. He grew more conscious of what was going on around him. He was getting fully involved in the ordinary, everyday miracles that were part of his life.

Knowing that whatever he experiences in life is what he brings to it, William could honestly say he was happy. He knew he didn't have all the answers. Of course, sometimes he still felt uncertain or fearful, but it no longer consumed his life. In fact, those experiences were increasingly becoming the exception. William was in love not just with Emily, he was in love with life!

The sound of a deep sigh rose from the foot of the boulder. He leaned out and looked down to see a man leaning wearily on the guard rail of the bridge. There was something familiar about the man's posture - the tense way he held his shoulders. William nodded sympathetically. It reminded him of himself, not so long ago.

"Hello," he said quietly. Startled, the man looked around for the source of his voice. William raised his hand. "Up here."

"Oh. Hi. Thought I was hearing voices there for a minute."

"Only mine," William chuckled.

The fellow looked about uncertainly, like he might bolt at any moment.

"Nice view from up here, huh?" William said.

"Yeah, I guess. I'm new to the city... this place seemed like... a good place to... de-stress," he answered, rolling head to shoulder, attempting to relax tight muscles. You live around here?"

"Naw, I just come here to meditate sometimes," William said.

"Meditate?" the man repeated distractedly.

"It's how I find peacefulness and clarity," William said. William noticed the guy's inner turmoil was nearly palpable. "A way to relax and deal with stress..."

"I could use some of that," he said with a weary sigh. "I've been struggling a lot lately," he added. Looking a little embarrassed, he quickly changed the subject. "So, what do you do?"

William grinned. "I'm into metaphysical electronics..."